T0383729

China's Digital Civilization

This book focuses on the "algorithmic turn" in state surveillance and the development of new platforms that allow the Chinese Communist Party (CCP) to shape human behavior in all areas of life through its widespread social credit system.

Perhaps no country has gone further than China in setting up overt systematic tracking, surveillance and constant computational evaluation of its citizens. Everyday life is saturated with a pervasive digitization that affects social mobility, economic opportunities and personal freedoms. Global organizations operating in China have to take account of the ramifications of these systems for data protection within the CCP's explicit project of forming a digital civilization. The volume covers the new technological practices that have transformed how states acquire and analyze personal data, the "TikTok-ification" of society as social credit platforms built on the familiarity with this popular app's interaction paradigm and the fast expansion of the digital economy that followed the new legal status of data as a production component in 2019.

Scholars and students from many backgrounds, as well as policy makers, journalists and the general reading public, will find a multidisciplinary approach to questions posed by research into China's digital civilization project from media, journalism, communication and global studies.

Michael Filimowicz is Senior Lecturer in the School of Interactive Arts and Technology (SIAT) at Simon Fraser University. He has a background in computer-mediated communications, audiovisual production, new media art and creative writing. His research develops new multimodal display technologies and forms, exploring novel form factors across different application contexts including gaming, immersive exhibitions and simulations.

Algorithms and Society
Series Editor
Dr Michael Filimowicz
Senior Lecturer in the School of Interactive Arts and Technology (SIAT) at Simon Fraser University.

As algorithms and data flows increasingly penetrate every aspect of our lives, it is imperative to develop sufficient theoretical lenses and design approaches to humanize our informatic devices and environments. At stake are the human dimensions of society which stand to lose ground to calculative efficiencies and performance, whether at the service of government, capital, criminal networks, or even a general mob concatenated in social media.

Algorithms and Society is a new series which takes a broad view of the information age. Each volume focuses on an important thematic area, from new fields such as software studies and critical code studies to more established areas of inquiry such as philosophy of technology and science and technology studies. This series aims to stay abreast of new areas of controversy and social issues as they emerge with the development of new technologies.

If you wish to submit a book proposal for the series, please contact Dr Michael Filimowicz michael_f@sfu.ca or Emily Briggs emily.briggs@tandf.co.uk

Algorithmic Ethics
Algorithms and Society
Edited by Michael Filimowicz

China's Digital Civilization
Algorithms and Society
Edited by Michael Filimowicz

Decolonizing Data
Algorithms and Society
Edited by Michael Filimowicz

Information Disorder
Algorithms and Society
Edited by Michael Filimowicz

For more information on the series, visit: www.routledge.com/Algorithms-and-Society/book-series/ALGRAS

China's Digital Civilization

Algorithms and Society

Edited by Michael Filimowicz

LONDON AND NEW YORK

First published 2023
by Routledge
4 Park Square, Milton Park, Abingdon, Oxon OX14 4RN

and by Routledge
605 Third Avenue, New York, NY 10158

Routledge is an imprint of the Taylor & Francis Group, an informa business

British Library Cataloguing-in-Publication Data
A catalogue record for this book is available from the British Library

Library of Congress Cataloging-in-Publication Data
Names: Filimowicz, Michael, editor.
Title: China's digital civilization : algorithms and society / edited by Michael Filimowicz.
Description: Abingdon, Oxon ; New York, NY : Routledge, 2023. |
    Series: Algorithms and society | Includes bibliographical references
    and index.
Identifiers: LCCN 2023009435 (print) | LCCN 2023009436 (ebook) |
    ISBN 9781032290683 (hardback) | ISBN 9781032290683 (paperback) |
    ISBN 9781003299899 (ebook)
Subjects: LCSH: Internet—Social aspects—China. | Privacy, Right of—
    China. | Electronic surveillance—China. | Technology and state—China.
Classification: LCC HN740.Z9 I5629 2024 (print) | LCC HN740.Z9 (ebook) |
    DDC 302.23/10951—dc23/eng/20230417
LC record available at https://lccn.loc.gov/2023009435
LC ebook record available at https://lccn.loc.gov/2023009436

ISBN: 978-1-032-29068-3 (hbk)
ISBN: 978-1-032-29069-0 (pbk)
ISBN: 978-1-003-29989-9 (ebk)

DOI: 10.4324/9781003299899

Typeset in Times New Roman
by Apex CoVantage, LLC

Contents

Contributors

Brett Aho is a Ph.D. candidate at the University of California Santa Barbara, where he specializes in global political economy and comparative regulatory politics. His return to academia follows a meandering career as a journalist and consultant in Washington, DC, and Brussels. His current research focuses on the governance of artificial intelligence and big data technologies in the United States, the EU and China. A former Fulbright recipient, he has previously earned degrees from the University of Leipzig, Roskilde University and the University of Redlands, and also serves as managing editor for the *Journal of Environment and Development*.

Yi Guo (Ph.D., Macquarie University) is Associate Professor and the Head of the Department of International Communication in the School of Journalism and Communication at Chongqing University in China. He is the author of *Freedom of the Press in China: A Conceptual History* (Amsterdam University Press, 2020). Guo has published peer-reviewed articles in English-language journals such as *Javnost—The Public*, *Media History*, and the *International Journal of Comic Art*, among others.

Fan Liang (Ph.D., University of Michigan) is Assistant Professor of Media in the Division of Social Sciences at Duke Kunshan University. His research explores how new communication technologies construct social and political changes, and how social and political powers shape and regulate the design and operation of such technologies. His research has received recognition and support from American Council of Learned Societies (ACLS), British Foreign, Commonwealth and Development Office, International Communication Association and other organizations.

Leiyuan Tian is a Media and Arts (History) major from the Undergraduate Class of 2023 at Duke Kunshan University. Her research explores ways of understanding new media and digital communication, with a focus on online fandoms and marginalized communities.

Series Preface

Algorithms and Society

Michael Filimowicz

This series is less about what algorithms are and more about how they act in the world through "eventful" (Bucher, 2018, p. 48) forms of "automated decision making" (Noble, 2018, loc. 141) in which computational models are "based on choices made by fallible human beings" (O'Neil, 2016, loc. 126).

> Decisions that used to be based on human refection are now made automatically. Software encodes thousands of rules and instructions computed in a fraction of a second.
>
> (Pasquale, 2015, loc. 189)

> If, in the industrial era, the promise of automation was to displace manual labor, in the information age it is to pre-empt agency, spontaneity, and risk: to map out possible futures before they hap-pen so objectionable ones can be foreclosed and desirable ones selected.
>
> (Andrejevic, 2020, p. 8)

> [M]achine learning algorithms that anticipate our future propensities are seriously threatening the chances that we have to make possible alternative political futures.
>
> (Amoore, 2020, p. xi)

Algorithms, definable pragmatically as "a method for solving a problem" (Finn, 2017, loc. 408), "leap from one feld to the next" (O'Neil, 2016, loc. 525). They are "hyperobjects: things with such broad temporal and spatial reach that they exceed the phenomenological horizon of human subjects" (Hong, 2020, p. 30). While in the main, the techno-logical systems taken up as volume topics are design solutions to problems for which there are commercial markets, organized communities, or claims of state interest, their power and ubiquity generate new problems for inquiry. The series will do its part to track this domain fuidity across its volumes and contest, through critique and investigation, their "logic of secrecy" (Pasquale, 2015, loc. 68), and "obfuscation" (loc. 144).

These new social (rather than strictly computational) problems that are generated can, in turn, be taken up by many critical, policy, and speculative discourses. At their most productive, such debates can potentially alter the ethical, legal, and even imaginative parameters of the environments in which the algorithms of our information architectures and infrastructures operate, as algorithmic implementations often reflect a "desire for epistemic purity, of knowledge stripped of uncertainty and human guesswork" (Hong, 2020, p. 20). The series aims to foster a general intervention in the conversation around these often "black boxed" technologies and track their pervasive effects in society.

> Contemporary algorithms are not so much transgressing settled societal norms as establishing new patterns of good and bad, new thresholds of normality and abnormality, against which actions are calibrated.
>
> (Amoore, 2020, p. 5)

Less "hot button" algorithmic topics are also of interest to the series, such as their use in the civil sphere by citizen scientists, activists, and hobbyists, where there is usually not as much discursive attention. Beyond private, state, and civil interests, the increasingly sophisticated technology-based activities of criminals, whether amateur or highly organized, deserve broader attention as now everyone must defend their digital identities. The information systems of companies and states conduct a general form of "ambient surveillance" (Pasquale, 2015, loc. 310), and anyone can be a target of a hacking operation.

Algorithms and Society thus aims to be an interdisciplinary series which is open to researchers from a broad range of academic back-grounds. While each volume has its defined scope, chapter contributions may come from many areas such as sociology, communications, critical legal studies, criminology, digital humanities, economics, computer science, geography, computational media and design, philosophy of technology, and anthropology, along with others. Algorithms are "shaping the conditions of everyday life" (Bucher, 2018, p. 158) and operate "at the intersection of computational space, cultural systems, and human cognition" (Finn, 2017, loc. 160), so the multidisciplinary terrain is vast indeed. Since the series is based on the shorter Routledge Focus format, it can be nimble and responsive to emerging areas of debate in fast-changing technological domains and their sociocultural impacts.

References

Amoore, L. (2020). *Cloud ethics: Algorithms and the attributes of ourselves and others.* Duke University Press.
Andrejevic, M. (2020). *Automated media.* Taylor and Francis.

Bucher, T. (2018). *If. . . Then: Algorithmic power and politics.* Oxford University Press.

Finn, E. (2017). *What algorithms want: Imagination in the age of computing.* MIT Press. Kindle version.

Hong, S. H. (2020). *Technologies of speculation: The limits of knowledge in a data-driven society.* New York University Press.

Noble, S. U. (2018). *Algorithms of oppression.* New York University Press. Kindle version.

O'Neil, C. (2016). *Weapons of math destruction.* Broadway Books. Kindle version.

Pasquale, F. (2015). *The black box society.* Harvard University Press. Kindle version.

Volume Introduction

Perhaps no country has gone further than China in setting up overt systematic tracking, surveillance and constant computational evaluation of its citizens. Everyday life is saturated with a pervasive digitization that affects social mobility, economic opportunities and personal freedoms. Global organizations operating in China have to take account of the ramifications of these systems for data protection within the CCP's explicit project of forming a digital civilization.

Chapter 1—"From Citizens to Users: The Algorithmic Turn in China's Surveillance Apparatus" by Fan Liang and Leiyuan Tian—explores the new technological practices that have transformed how states acquire and analyze personal data by examining the recent shifts in China's citizen surveillance. The "algorithmic turn" uses interactive digital technology to move beyond the panopticon tradition that has dominated surveillance discourse. Now, citizens themselves are active users of surveillance platforms, generating personal data and monitoring their own and peers' activities, as platform mechanisms like gamification are increasingly incorporated in China's surveillance techniques. The new "participatory" surveillance maintains the power imbalance between observer and watched, defining the new monitoring methods being developed by the state and the tech industry it increasingly, and more explicitly, controls. In this instance, bottom-up involvement by citizens is not freely participatory but limited to movement within strict power-hierarchy structures.

Chapter 2—"The TikTok-ification of Chinese Society" by Yi Guo—observes that as the digital industry expands in Chinese sociopolitical settings, Chinese media culture and lifestyle are becoming more like TikTok. TikTok, which just surpassed Google as the most popular online platform, is considered by many as changing how social media operates in society. As a sign of China's unfinished but continuous project of "digital civilization," the trends analyzed by the author help us envisage what the ramifications of this process may imply for China and the rest of the world. New concerns are emerging as many are prepared to accept the TikTok-ification of society as readily as they accept TikTok itself because of their familiarity with its interaction paradigms. This is a particularly worrying aspect of the problem that needs to be further researched. The TikTok-ification of Chinese culture is a form of "soft control" like that used by the government to preserve its popularity and position in people's daily lives, establishing a more restrictive culture by making everyone more "transparent" to the authorities.

Chapter 3—"Toward an Algorithmically Planned Economy: Data Policy and the Digital Restructuring of China" by Brett Aho—analyzes the acceleration in China's digital growth that occurred after data was legally acknowledged as a production component in 2019. With a slew of new rules, the government is asserting its power over the IT sector and positioning itself to regulate the nation's data flows. The government's goals include boosting data supply and its circulation as it hastens a move from high-speed to high-quality economic growth. Data supervision is increasingly crucial to the creation of China's social credit system (SCS), a novel regulatory framework that algorithmically coordinates aspects of general economic activity. China has taken unprecedented moves to govern how emerging technologies are integrated into society, and its nondemocratic, authoritarian power systems have allowed it to shape its data revolution ahead at a faster pace than in most countries.

Michael Filimowicz

Acknowledgment

The chapter summaries here have in places drawn from the authors' chapter abstracts, the full versions of which can be found in Routledge's online reference for the volume.

1 From Citizens to Users

The Algorithmic Turn in China's Surveillance Apparatus

Fan Liang and Leiyuan Tian

Introduction

Recent years have witnessed significant transformations in how states and private sectors extract personal data and monitor individual behaviors due to the rapid development of information and communication technologies (ICTs) (Cheney-Lippold, 2017; Lyon, 2015). Historically, authorities adopted human labor to collect population-level statistics, making it impossible to continuously track individual citizens (Taylor et al., 2007). The use of advanced technologies, particularly algorithms and big data, has enabled new ways of seeing and assessing individuals (Andrejevic & Gates, 2014). Scholars have examined the unprecedented practice of gathering and exploiting personal data from various perspectives, such as surveillance (Gates, 2011), digital platforms (Van Dijck, 2014) and identities (Cheney-Lippold, 2017). However, we know little about how new technologies shape and change those who are watched and monitored in the surveillance systems.

In this chapter, we explore how the changing dynamics of ICTs are feeding into the ongoing shifts and innovations in China's citizen surveillance apparatus. Focusing on three cases of algorithm-driven surveillance (i.e., Health Code, Xuexi Qiangguo and Zhima Credit), this chapter demonstrates that individuals are encouraged by states to actively participate in surveillance practices, and meanwhile, surveillance moves forward to the practice of microtargeting, prediction, and gamification. Our findings suggest that algorithms have profoundly transformed citizens to platform users and further facilitated participatory surveillance. Both states and citizens rely increasingly on digital platforms to engage in surveillance, and more importantly, platform mechanisms such as datafication and gamification have been widely embedded in China's surveillance practices. These transformations, which we term "algorithmic turn," routinely take advantage of the interactive features of digital technologies to update surveillance practices that move beyond the panopticon tradition which has long held the dominating role in citizen surveillance. As a result, new technologies raise the possibility of a fundamental shift in state surveillance: the subjects of surveillance are no longer passive

DOI: 10.4324/9781003299899-1

citizens who are watched by the architectural design of the panopticon; they are instead platform users who actively participate in mass surveillance by generating personal data and monitoring their own and peers' behaviors. This chapter proceeds as follows. We first review previous scholarship on surveillance and citizen classification. Our review shows that the practice of classifying and categorizing citizens has shifted into automated approaches. Next, we briefly introduce the cases used in this chapter, as well as China's surveillance systems in the pre-digital age. In our theoretical framework, we propose that the shift from citizens to users can be configured into three components: the emphasis on participation, the practice of microtargeting and prediction, and the use of gamification. Our results demonstrate that these three components have been deeply integrated into China's surveillance apparatus.

Citizen Classification: Sorting People In and Out

Surveillance involves a range of practices exhibiting traits of "purposeful, routine, systematic and focused attention paid to personal details, for the sake of control, entitlement, management, influence or protection" (Wood et al., 2006, p. 4). In other words, surveillance is a structured observation and collection of individual data planned for taking control and/or care of the subjects. This definition thus encompasses various approaches conceptualizing surveillance following a theoretical evolution over time, from Bentham's panopticons and Foucault's disciplinary society to Deleuze's control society, Haggerty and Ericson's surveillant assemblage, Clarke's dataveillance, Lyon's social sorting and so on. Meanwhile, what we meant by "subjects" of surveillance are beyond passive actors but expand to include those who actively participate in the implementation of surveillance measures. This transformation in understandings of agency in surveillance societies is reflected in contemporary scholarships, such as lateral surveillance (Andrejevic, 2002) and participatory surveillance (Albrechtslund, 2008).

Early scholarly scrutiny of surveillance could be found in Foucault's concept of panopticism, which is rooted in Bentham's panopticon penitentiary and in direct reference to the "prison-Panopticon" prototype (Galič et al., 2016). The quintessential panopticon is an enclosed circular architectural apparatus that renders each peripheral inhabitant conspicuous while being constantly exposed to inspection from concealed supervisors in the central tower (Božovič, 2010; Miller & Miller, 1987). The apparatus could be appropriated for different uses, including managing pauper populations, schooling the youth and even in an inverted variation, allowing the public to supervise the government (Brunon-Ernst, 2013; Mosse & Whitley, 2009). Through the subtle discipling process of generating and internalizing social norms, individuals become docile bodies that seldom deviate from normative types, while deviant behaviors are subjected to surveillance that identifies and governs thoroughly the society (Foucault, 1991).

In this chapter, we pay particular attention to one of the major practices of surveillance—classification (or social sorting)—to explore how the use of algorithms reshapes state surveillance in China. Generally, classification refers to "a spatial, temporal, or spatiotemporal segmentation of the world" (Bowker & Star, 2000b, p. 149). For the purpose of this chapter, we will use surveillance and classification interchangeably to indicate the categorization and quantification of individuals. Through classification, people and things are defined, separated, ordered and finally sorted out (Bowker & Star, 2000a). They are classified by a variety of classification schemes, such as gender, ethnicity, class and employability (Garsten & Jacobsson, 2013). Consequently, states can determine who should be targeted for access, eligibility, suspicion or exclusion (Lyon, 2007). Admittedly, classification, or social sorting, is one of the oldest and powerful tools used by state actors for the political reduction of social complexity (Starr, 1992). States often adopt classification to achieve institutional purposes like citizenship identification, crime control, law enforcements, welfare and surveillance (Bowker & Star, 2000a). For instance, European nations have long-standing practices of identifying and categorizing citizens since the sixteenth century (Marx, 2016). The classification of individuals created the docile person (Foucault, 1991) and reflected existing social structures (Durkheim & Mauss, 1969). The rise of welfare states further facilitates administrative classification, social sorting and the national census by collecting detailed personal information and offering separate public services (Lips et al., 2009).

Furthermore, classification is not natural or given. Instead, it is embedded with organizational and bureaucratic knowledge structures, aiming to reduce complexities and create distinctions between individuals (Boyne, 2006; Diedrich et al., 2011). Thus, classification generates ways of seeing and knowing people and decides whether people can access public services or people are at risk (Bowker & Star, 2000a; Garsten & Jacobsson, 2013). Notably, the process of classifying citizens is related to administrative and structural systems (Diedrich et al., 2011; Starr, 1992). By citizens' classification, states avoid treating individuals as unique objects and transform social structures into schemes and categories. Meanwhile, classification remains largely invisible to the population (Bowker & Star, 2000a). As such, the bureaucratic classification practices have become social agreements that maintain social orders and cultivate and restrict individual behavior and thinking (Bowker & Star, 2000a; Diedrich et al., 2011).

The Development of Algorithmic Classification

Traditionally, citizen classification was associated with paper-based administration and human assessment (Lips et al., 2009). Personal information like name, address and birthplace was collected by government officials for identification and authentication. Normally, a civil servant evaluated the paper record according to administrative classification categories and determined the eligibility of individuals (Taylor et al., 2007). Individuals then received document-based identification, such as passport, ID card and driver's license, in order to access public services and welfares. Thus, citizen classification was labor intensive and could take considerable time, and personal information was stored separately within each government department (Lips et al., 2009; Marx, 2016).

The deployment of new communication technologies is increasingly transforming the conventional classification to algorithm-based systems. Deleuze (1992) identified the shift in direct subjects of surveillance from individuals to their numerical representations, which enables live tracking for "rapid rates of turn-over" and ceaseless calculations for constant control (p. 6). New tools also facilitate the heterogenization of agents and approaches to exercise surveillance, as reflected in Haggerty and Ericson (2000)'s proposal of the "surveillant assemblage" to capture the opaque flows of surveillance practices and technologies across institutions. The expansive nature of such a volatile device thus enables surveillance to transcend spatial confinements of panoptic archetypes. Meanwhile, bodies are first abstracted from contexts and then reassembled into "data doubles," virtual profiles that are sold, manipulated and used in the interests of both state and non-state institutions (Haggerty & Ericson, 2000). Moreover, Clarke (1988) draws attention to the transformative role of ICTs in shaping contemporary surveillance by introducing the term "dataveillance." The concept highlights automation as a distinctive characteristic of digital monitoring systems that ameliorates the inspector's invisibility and omnipresence, further obscuring the intelligibility of surveillance to the subjects (Clarke, 2003). Examples of this data-based surveillance practices include closed-circuit television (CCTV), interactive media and the internet.

More recently, technologies like electronic identification system are increasingly used for improving identification and classification (van Dijck & Jacobs, 2019). The government and digital platforms also provide centralized information infrastructures and online identity services to collect, sort and classify personal data (Zuboff, 2019). Consequently, state actors can easily capture large amounts of data about individuals and aggregate information for microtargeting and automating classification. A growing body of literature reveals that the classification process has been significantly embedded into algorithms and information infrastructures for creating new forms of administrative sorting (Andrejevic & Gates, 2014).

Although the use of personal data for surveillance is nothing new, the advent of algorithms and big data has produced an exponential increase in the depth and the scope of data used for surveillance, thereby amplifying surveillance of citizens by state and private sectors (Andrejevic, 2019). Indeed, algorithms and big data innovations have been regarded as crucial tools of social control in many countries, including the United States, the United

Kingdom, Canada and China (Lyon, 2015). For example, both democratic countries and authoritarian regimes have doubled their surveillance investments since 2006, and this dramatic change is strongly associated with the technological revolutions in big data and cloud computing (Kostyuk et al., 2017). In addition to the increase in surveillance practices, algorithms and big data have the potential to intensify the way by which surveillance system functions. Scholars in communication, sociology, political science and criminology have noted the significance of big data and computing for contemporary surveillance (Lyon, 2015; Van Dijck, 2014).

Currently, the classification system has largely become an automated process entrenched in institutional infrastructures (Gandy, 2012). While paper-based classification was mainly dependent upon separate and incomplete information about individual *status*, automated classification enables state institutions to aggregate comprehensive and continuous information about the *status* and *activities* of individuals from various sources (Andrejevic & Gates, 2014). The collect-everything approach has facilitated microtargeting and real-time categorization (Andrejevic, 2019). As such, states can place citizens within a multidimensional space, aiming to not only identify "who you are" but also evaluate "what you are" (Gandy, 2012, p. 126). In addition, current classification relies on algorithmically supported decision-making rather than human assessment (Andrejevic & Gates, 2014). Thus, individuals are assessed and classified in the context of statistical estimation, and human agency is further transformed to algorithms and statistical analytics (Cheney-Lippold, 2017).

From Citizens to Users

In this section, we examine the algorithmic turn of China's surveillance from three aspects: the shift to participation, the emphasis on prediction and microtargeting, and the gamification of classification. As discussed in the following, these aspects provide a theoretical framework to understand the current state surveillance in China enabled by algorithms and big data. Moreover, we will use three cases to analyze how the adoption of algorithms considerably reshapes and transforms China's surveillance. The first case is China's Health Code, a platform-based contact-tracing application used to detect people's exposure to COVID-19 and their freedom of movement in early 2020 (Liang, 2020). It is a collaboration between the Chinese government and two major platforms Alipay and WeChat. The Health Code was no longer required since the end of 2022 when China changed its zero-COVID policy. The second case is China's propaganda platform Xuexi Qiangguo which aims to assess and quantify people's information exposure and political learning (Liang et al., 2021). This platform is designed to convent algorithmic logic into state propaganda and classification apparatus. Finally, we discuss Zhima Credit on Alipay and how people understand this crediting platform. As a commercial crediting system, Zhima Credit offers real-time monitoring of users' online transactions (Chong, 2019). Meanwhile, it has been rapidly used to facilitate participatory and peer-to-peer surveillance.

Pre-digital Surveillance in China

The collection and analysis of personal data has a long history in the People's Republic of China (PRC). The government has implemented multiple systems to identify and classify its citizens in terms of classes, households and occupations. *Dang'an*, for instance, was originally designed in the Mao era to expand personal profiling and management (Zhang, 2004). The system gathers personnel dossiers to record information about people's education, occupations, family background, administrative reward and punishment, and so on. *Dang'an* focused mainly on urban and industrial areas, and is particularly important for Party cadres, as it is often used to assess the performance of individuals in China (Moss, 1996).

Another system *Hukou* was developed in the 1950s for population registration and regulation in China. In addition to simply collecting personal information, *Hukou* enables the government to monitor mobility and identify personal status (Chan & Zhang, 1999). *Hukou* can determine whether people are eligible for various activities in urban areas. Those who do not have a *Hukou* in cities, for example, are often excluded from accessing certain public and commercial activities, such as education and health.

From Panopticon to Participation

The architectural design of the panopticon is an arrangement of power relations: with the inspector positioned at the center and the inmates at the peripheral, the active and dominant role is designated to the concealed former while participation from the visible latter is only passive. Thus, surveillance scholars presume that individuals being monitored are forced to be involved and only reactive to what becomes exercised upon them (Albrechtslund & Glud, 2010). As a result, studies on pre-digital surveillance focused almost exclusively on structural designs and implications of the surveillant systems as well as those who operate the systems, yet little attention has been paid to the agency of targets of surveillance. However, the interactivity of digital practices has invited reflections on the issue. Active engagement in surveillance on digital platforms deviates from models of hierarchical relationships that once seemed unnegotiable. User-generated surveillance, including mutual and self-surveillance, characterizes this nascent form of mass participation in surveillance through the widespread use of digital media.

In contrast to the hierarchical understanding of surveillance, Albrechtslund (2008) argues for the emergence of a mutual, horizontal alternative on social networking sites that engages users in "participatory surveillance," the voluntary contribution of personal information undefined by unbalanced power relations. Disclosing personal data such as profiles and status on social networking sites is understood as a practice of active sharing that empowers individuals to express their identities and communicate with peers. Therefore, participatory surveillance motivates user engagement for the articulation of individuality and the enjoyment of social interactions (Albrechtslund, 2013). Moreover, Alberschtslund's proposition was set in dialogue with an opposing view that sees interactivity as an deceptive promise of grassroot empowerment, especially Andrejevic's notion of lateral surveillance and automating surveillance (Andrejevic, 2002, 2019). Drawing on the concept of "responsibilization" from theories of risk society, Andrejevic (2002) understands the invitation to participate in peer monitoring as a deliberate dissemination of responsibilities to individuals that eases the burden for state and commercial entities to identify and harvest personal data. Delegating tasks of watching each other to a member of a community also reinforces norms and beliefs about what constitutes a well-behaved and accountable individual, thus persuading participants to agree with the core values of and justifications for the system.

Admittedly, China's surveillance programs initiated by the government in collaboration with tech giants like Tencent and Alibaba remain the most influential players in the game. Most commonly, platforms such as WeChat and Alipay act as the widely accessible platforms for individual participation in these top-down programs. The surveillant assemblage thus becomes platformized, where participation could be read as user interaction and the rules of personal data trade translated to terms of service. By navigating platforms that visualize and concretize the experience of daily surveillance, users come to recognize the contours of the data-powered surveillance machine and make sense of how it works and why it exists. Therefore, examining this user-platform relationship can shed light on the digital practices performed by Chinese citizens in everyday life that constitute indispensable parts of China's surveillance systems.

Typically, platforms purposed for surveillance ask for both identification information and regular updates from the users. Take Health Code as an example. As mentioned, Health Code refers to an ensemble of regional and national public health tracking apps developed by the Chinese government and tech firms to contain the COVID-19 outbreak in early 2020, which requires individuals to not only provide their ID number and biometric data (e.g., facial recognition) but also report their travel history and health status. Although Health Code automatically collects geolocation data by tracking users' smartphones across the nation and even internationally, users must manually update their travel and health information in order to maintain a green code for free mobility. This practice termed "individual declaration, individual authorization" indicates the authorities' attempt to delegate responsibilities for health monitoring to citizen-users. Yet there appears to be certain ambiguity in the framing of inquiries for information and a lack of rigorous fact-checking of self-reported data. For example, users were asked to report if they had contact with individuals showing suspicious symptoms, to which most would be motivated to answer "no," as it is convenient to deny the possibility when recollections of such occurrences fail to surface.

The relaxed supervision over the accuracy of self-reports via Health Code reflects degrees of flexibility in China's pandemic management as well as a shift from restrictive to affirmative in the direction of social control achieved through surveillance. In other words, surveillance is no longer solely tied up with measures of restricting access to information and services but transforming toward shaping modes of behavior by recommending and guiding. While citizens entrust the government to use their data for public interests, the government also depends on the cooperation of citizens to truthfully present inquired information. Moreover, being honest is not enough. Paired with patriotic propaganda and national media coverage of severe situations caused by the COVID-19, China's state-launched surveillance programs have been persuading citizens to internalize a sense of social responsibility and modify their risk perception accordingly, especially in situations like the pandemic where risky behaviors and persons of risk are difficult to define. Therefore, the aforementioned request of contact self-report is both an attempt to "responsiblize" individuals and a test on citizen spirits—a model citizen should never underestimate the potential risk of missing any incident of suspicion and risk harming the general good.

However, user behavior should not be understood as only evolving in accordance with platforms' intentions. Instead of acting precisely as anticipated, citizen-users have invented participatory paths into the surveillant architecture by fabricating social contexts and alternative uses around the types of data abstracted from them. For example, while Zhima Credits is designed as an evaluative system of financial credibility whose score calculation is affected by personal economic activities tracked on Alipay, users have appropriated it to serve as referential points of trustworthiness in various digital scenarios of social interactions. To prove themselves and check others' credibility, some users would voluntarily show their Zhima scores or ask others for their scores when they seek friendship or romantic relationships online. Although higher scores seem to yield little marginal gain to the positive impression of an online stranger, below-average scores are often viewed as red flags indicating dishonesty and deviancy. In fact, lower scores could result from unintended, banal actions such as forgetting to return shared power banks.

In China, the robust expansion in mobile media has subsequently led to an integration of mutual watching into everyday practices, particularly among urban populations with higher rates of digital literacy. When it comes to participatory surveillance, the increasingly popular practice of broadcasting personal updates and exchanging opinions on social media has been obscuring the boundaries between the private and the public, rendering acts of watching and being watched less invasive but playful and socially rewarding. Moreover, despite strict censorship over online posts, photos and videos captured with phone cameras have helped transmit the power of witnessing and justice-seeking to hands of less privileged citizens. The panoptic metaphor seems to have turned obsolete in the presence of diverse actors consciously and voluntarily gathering, utilizing and sharing data about each other on a level playing field. In fact, these practices do not take place on Alipay but on other platforms like Weibo and WeChat that afford social interactions. While the original platform fails to facilitate this type of participatory surveillance, users have been able to repurpose the data generated for surveillance on social platforms where participation occurs more easily and naturally. In cross-platform contexts, the juxtaposition of participatory practices with peer-to-peer and self-monitoring can be widely observed in many cases of digital surveillance in China. Therefore, even within hierarchies of power, Chinese users have been exploring "flat" spaces of open participation that allow for approaching surveillance as alternative entertainment and socialization.

Microtargeting and Prediction

One of the major differences between algorithm-enabled classification and the previous one is that the former concentrates on data-driven microtargeting and prediction to manipulate and control individuals. Traditionally, surveillance methods attempted to target populations and groups of people. As mentioned, China's *Hukou* systems can assess the mobility of rural residents to include or exclude those who have rural *Hukou*. Yet it is difficult to conduct real-time tracking of individuals using *Hukou*. In addition, another feature of old surveillance is that its approaches were retrospective, meaning that they were dealing with past events (Lyon, 2007). What traditional surveillance did, thus, was to identify the events and then punish those who were watched.

By contrast, current surveillance systems are capable of microtargeting individuals while simultaneously predicting their behaviors. First, the collection of massive data from individuals means that algorithmic surveillance aims to make individuals readable and processable. As a result, the system has the potential to identify specific persons and link their online behaviors with offline data. The unprecedented data gathering suggests that almost all aspects of individual behaviors have been monitored and assessed by algorithms embedded in citizen classification. More importantly, the new system enables real-time data collection and analytics, meaning that it can generate timely evaluations and predict people's behaviors. This has significantly altered the way in which citizens are monitored and classified by surveillance approaches.

One example of microtargeting and prediction is Health Code. The idea of Health Code is to continuously assess and then predict individuals' exposure risk. A color-based code (Green, Yellow and Red) will be assigned to each user, determining their health status and freedom of movement. Moreover, individuals must provide Health Code with their personal data, including ID number, travel history and biometric data, and keep them up to date. This allows Health Code to target each person and then monitor their daily activities. In addition, Health Code also collects geolocation data from users' smartphones to evaluate whether people have visited "risk" areas. Next, Health Code aggregates all personal data and generates a color-based code for each user to indicate people's exposure risks and freedom of movement. In this process, Health Code examines very detailed information of each person in order to track and assess exposure risks. Compared to conventional contact-tracing methods, Health Code can instantly and continually watch people's offline behaviors and then generate a simplified code for them.

Furthermore, Health Code can predict whether individuals are at risks, which is achieved through connecting users' data with existing pandemic surveillance information. For example, a person's Health Code will be automatically changed to red, meaning that this person has high exposure risk and thus needs to self-quarantine, if he/she traveled to risk areas and/or contacted with confirmed cases. While it is obvious that persons who obtain a red code are not always at risk of exposure, Health Code forecasts that they have a higher chance of contracting COVID-19. The prediction of Health Code suggests that citizen classification can be used by the government and tech giants to systematically assess and then predict people's possibility of risks. This has changed the retroactive principle fixed in traditional classification infrastructures. Moreover, this also indicates that individuals need to deal with increased uncertainty and monitoring, because they will be increasingly microtargeted and their future behaviors and outcomes will be evaluated by surveillance.

However, there have been concerns regarding the implementation of microtargeting and prediction in citizens classification. First, microtargeting relies heavily on the aggregation of online and offline data, but those who lack digital skills and internet access may not be able to provide enough data for identification and microtargeting. For instance, it has been found that some elderlies were unable to use Health Code as they did not have smartphones. Also, some people fabricated personal information in order to bypass Health Code's microtargeting. Second, prediction does not necessarily mean accuracy, since most people who obtained red code were not infected. Instead, the prediction function could be used by local governments for other purposes such as social management and control. In July 2022, some people found that their Health Code had turned red, even though they had not left their cities. The reason was that they were depositors of rural banks in Henan province who fought against the rural banking scandal. It turns out that the local government changed these depositors' Health Code to stop them from going to Henan to protest, because people with the red code cannot travel. This case suggests that, although Health Code is a digital tool aimed at pandemic control, it can be easily utilized by other actors to control the mobility of citizens.

The Gamification of Surveillance

What is striking in the case of algorithmic surveillance is how people react to such systems that attempt to constantly watch their behaviors. In this section, we explore the gamification of China's surveillance practices to explain the transformation from citizens to users, as well as its consequences. We argue that algorithmic surveillance has deeply incorporated the idea of gamification into its infrastructural design to encourage active involvement and data collection. That is, people are informed that they need to earn scores (or code) by providing data and/or completing various tasks. As a result, those who are being watched begin to consider surveillance systems as games that they need to play, and classification itself leverages gamification to improve participatory surveillance, microtargeting and prediction.

Indeed, all these cases used in this chapter provide some kinds of gamification for individuals. For example, the propaganda app Xuexi Qiangguo generates a "study score" for each user, quantifying people's online behaviors. Users can complete 14 tasks to earn up to 59 points each day. We classify these into four groups: log-in, information learning, information engagement and political tests. First, users receive one point per day when they log in to Xuexi Qiangguo. Second, reading news articles and watching videos are other ways for users to gain points (one point/one article or one video). Additionally, if users read an article for at least two minutes or watch a video for at least three minutes, they can receive one extra point. A user may gain a maximum of 25 points through information learning each day. Third, information engagement means that users can obtain points by subscribing, sharing, archiving or commenting on content. Each user can earn a maximum of six points from this category. Finally, users can take tests on Xuexi Qiangguo, and their study scores will raise if they provide correct answers. They can obtain a maximum of 27 points per day by taking tests.

Furthermore, Xuexi Qiangguo ranks users based on their study scores. Users can check their national ranking and group ranking if they join local study groups on Xuexi Qiangguo. More importantly, we find that some users of the platform consider the study scores and ranking as a game, thereby actively playing the game in order to earn more points. For example, people would cheer their high scores and compete with their friends and family members. As such, users use study scores as a way to show their engagement with the platform. Additionally, users also frequently gamify quizzes on Xuexi Qiangguo. Many users indicated that they preferred competing with their relatives and friends to learn about politics through quizzes.

Moreover, users can commercialize their study scores on Xuexi Qiangguo. The platform has a shopping feature where users can exchange their points for a variety of products, such as books, groceries and data plans for smartphones. It also offers a range of offline advantages. For instance, users who have more than 1,000 scores can receive complimentary attraction tickets in Henan,

Jiangxi, Guangdong and Beijing. In addition, local governments compile red lists that honor those with higher ratings. Thus, those who regularly read the news and participate in quizzes would score higher, and local governments would classify them as "excellent citizens" because of this. This further motivates users to accumulate more points on Xuexi Qiangguo.

Another case Zhima Credit also shows the importance of gamification in the current practices of surveillance in China. Like Xuexi Qiangguo, Zhima Credit provides a credit score to assess the trustworthiness of each user. To calculate one's credit scores, Zhima Credit breaks down more than 1,000 variables into five categories. First, it examines the user profile, which contains information like the user's name, ID number, employment history and even asset statements. Second, credit history is the most crucial factor in determining credit ratings since it determines if consumers uphold their end of the bargain when using the site. Users must, for instance, fulfill commitments for Alipay services like hotels, ridesharing and rentals. Then, preferences and behaviors are centered on a range of transactional activities, including internet buying, bill-paying and money transfers. Next, behaviors and preferences focus on a variety of transactional activities, such as online shopping, bill payment and money transfers. Lastly, Zhima Credit also takes the size of social networks into account: those who have more friends on Alipay would receive higher credit scores.

Furthermore, Zhima Credit assigns ratings on a scale from 350 (the least trustworthy) to 950 (the most trustworthy). Obviously, it makes an effort to translate personal data into standardized metrics to evaluate who they are, what they purchase, how much they spend online, how frequently they use Alipay to pay bills and fulfill their contractual obligations and with whom they connect—to assess one's credibility and trustworthiness. Interestingly, many users view Zhima scores as the game's main objective and thus gather information on how algorithms work and the rules of the rating game. They also participate in a variety of activities that could improve their credit scores. We find that users are curious to know more about the financial measures and border restrictions of the rating algorithms. For example, users discuss and elaborate aspects that would raise credit ratings (such as trust-keeping habits) and those that would drop their scores through information searching and exchange (i.e., trust-breaking behaviors). In fact, the use of Alipay and loan repayment are frequently cited as crucial elements that could enhance Zhima Credit.

This suggests that people are urged to frequently review their online activities and modify their online networks and behaviors to raise their Zhima scores. Such responses frequently mirror the advice given by Zhima Credit on how to raise one's credit score. Even if some users express skepticism regarding the rating system, the majority of users have accepted such criteria and implemented them to analyze their own behaviors. Despite making on-time bill payments, one user claims his Zhima score has fallen. Others respond by questioning whether the people have continuously complied with the platform's guidelines. Obviously, the overall response to Zhima Credit's rating algorithms is acceptance and finding ways to play with them, even when there are unspoken norms governing user behaviors that may not be in the users' best interests. Individuals are instructed to refrain from making unneeded returns, for instance, as they have learned via discussions that doing so frequently is seen as a bad thing that will affect one's Zhima Credit. Knowing about these kinds of unspoken laws allows users to act in a certain way.

Importantly, people appear to celebrate when their scores rise, especially when they get higher scores (like 800), but they react negatively and grunt when their numbers fall. Users also highlight different benefits they gain from having higher Zhima credits. Many claim, for instance, that having credit scores higher than 650 has given them access to privileges like deposit-free bike-sharing facilities. They also talk about other kinds of advantages, such as free entrance to tourist destinations and open access to public libraries. It's common for people to share such happy experiences with tremendous pride.

Overall, the two cases show that playing the game is a reactive tactic of users. To do this, they must first be familiar with the rules and guidelines of rating algorithms on these platforms. Indeed, users are encouraged to learn how algorithmic surveillance functions, how their behaviors are quantified and how to increase their scores on these platforms. Moreover, users need to actively play the game in order to increase or maintain their scores. In other words, they take part in the surveillance practices, and this could in turn generate new data for future classification. Although some users have expressed concerns about gamification on these platforms, we find that most users tend to accept the game and make an attempt to increase their scores. This suggests that gamification has the potential to promote people's understanding of how surveillance works and, more crucially, to encourage and even compulsorily enforce adherence to algorithmic rules and guidelines.

Conclusion

As ICTs are becoming a crucial part of society and economy, state surveillance as a way of social sorting and classification has been remarkably updated and changed. This chapter examines such changes by focusing on the algorithmic turn of China's surveillance apparatus. We claim that the emergence of platforms has paved the way for a new type of participatory surveillance, in which citizens are increasingly viewed as platform users who must provide data and participate in the process of tracking and monitoring themselves. At the same time, people are engaged in quantification and gamification, and new forms of surveillance can continuously target and forecast individual activities. As such, these transformations not only provide a new way of watching people but also enable states and other actors to cultivate good citizens by reshaping and redefining social norms and expectations.

Notably, participatory surveillance does not imply that individuals are empowered by algorithms or that they can escape surveillance. Rather, it still has the asymmetrical power relations between the watcher and watched, and it indicates a new way designed by states and tech firms to enhance surveillance capacities. Although citizens could exercise mutual monitoring and self-disclosure on digital platforms developed for the execution of such public programs, it is difficult for them to identify these practices as intrinsically motivated since power relations clearly permeate the process. As such, the environment for bottom-up engagement is hardly participatory but contained within the units of individuals classified into the same hierarchy of power. Echoing the idea of lateral surveillance (Andrejevic, 2002), this suggests that state and private sectors still preserve the power of watching over when the interactive means of surveillance have saved space for citizens to negotiate their roles inside the system.

The use of algorithms and data also challenge traditional surveillance methods and raise new problems. For example, every province has its own Health Code, and this decentralization and fragmentation indicate that personal data are not shared across local governments. Another concern is related to privacy and data security, which may prevent individuals from offering data for surveillance. Moreover, people's participation does not necessarily mean that they internalize social norms and values embedded in surveillance practices. Instead, people can trick the algorithmic systems by offering fake data. Thus, this may add complexity to the existing research that explores the role of digital technologies in state surveillance.

References

Albrechtslund, A. (2008). Online social networking as participatory surveillance. *First Monday*, *13*(3). https://doi.org/10.5210/fm.v13i3.2142

Albrechtslund, A. (2013). New media and changing perceptions of surveillance. In J. Hartley, J. Burgess, & A. Bruns (Eds.), *A Companion to new media dynamics* (pp. 311–321). John Wiley & Sons.

Albrechtslund, A., & Glud, L. N. (2010). Empowering residents: A theoretical framework for negotiating surveillance technologies. *Surveillance & Society*, *8*(2), 235–250. https://doi.org/10.24908/ss.v8i2.3488

Andrejevic, M. (2002). The work of watching one another: Lateral surveillance, risk, and governance. *Surveillance & Society*, *2*(4), 479–497. https://doi.org/10.24908/ss.v2i4.3359

Andrejevic, M. (2019). Automating surveillance. *Surveillance & Society*, *17*(1/2), 7–13. https://doi.org/10.24908/ss.v17i1/2.12930

Andrejevic, M., & Gates, K. A. (2014). Big data surveillance: Introduction. *Surveillance & Society*, *12*(2), 185–196. https://doi.org/10.24908/ss.v12i2.5242

Bowker, G. C., & Star, S. L. (2000a). *Sorting things out: Classification and its consequences*. MIT Press.

Bowker, G. C., & Star, S. L. (2000b). Invisible mediators of action: Classification and the ubiquity of standards. *Mind, Culture, and Activity*, *7*(1–2), 147–163. https://doi.org/10.1080/10749039.2000.9677652

Boyne, R. (2006). Classification. *Theory, Culture & Society, 23*(2–3), 21–31. https:// doi.org/10.1177/0263276406062529

Božovič, M. (2010). Introduction: An utterly dark spot. In M. Božovič (Ed.), *The panopticon writings* (pp. 1–28). Verso Books.

Brunon-Ernst, A. (2013). Introduction. In A. Brunon-Ernst (Ed.), *Beyond Foucault: New perspectives on Bentham's panopticon* (pp. 1–16). Ashgate Publishing.

Chan, K. W., & Zhang, L. (1999). The hukou system and rural-urban migration in China: Processes and changes. *The China Quarterly, 160,* 818–855. https://doi. org/10.1017/S0305741000001351

Cheney-Lippold, J. (2017). *We are data.* New York University Press.

Chong, G. P. L. (2019). Cashless China: Securitization of everyday life through Alipay's social credit system—sesame credit. *Chinese Journal of Communication, 12*(3), 290–307. https://doi.org/10.1080/17544750.2019.1583261

Clarke, R. (1988). Information technology and dataveillance. *Communications of the ACM, 31*(5), 498–512. https://doi.org/10.1145/42411.42413

Clarke, R. (2003, March 31). *Dataveillance—15 years on.* www.rogerclarke.com. www.rogerclarke.com/DV/DVNZ03.html

Deleuze, G. (1992). Postscript on the societies of control. In D. Wilson & C. Norris (Eds.), *Surveillance, crime and social control* (pp. 35–39). Routledge.

Diedrich, A., Eriksson-Zetterquist, U., & Styhre, A. (2011). Sorting people out: The uses of one-dimensional classificatory schemes in a multi-dimensional world. *Culture & Organization, 17*(4), 271–292. https://doi.org/10.1080/14759551.2011.590305

Durkheim, E., & Mauss, M. (1969). *Primitive classification.* Routledge.

Foucault, M. (1991). *Discipline and punish: The birth of the prison.* Vintage Books.

Galič, M., Timan, T., & Koops, B.-J. (2016). Bentham, Deleuze and beyond: An overview of surveillance theories from the panopticon to participation. *Philosophy & Technology, 30*(1), 9–37. https://doi.org/10.1007/s13347-016-0219-1

Gandy Jr, O. H. (2012). Statistical surveillance. In K. Ball, D. Lyon, & K. D. Haggerty (Eds.), *Routledge handbook of surveillance studies* (pp. 125–132). Routledge.

Garsten, C., & Jacobsson, K. (2013). Sorting people in and out: The plasticity of the categories of employability, work capacity and disability as technologies of government. *Ephemera, 13*(4), 825–850.

Gates, K. A. (2011). *Our biometric future: Facial recognition technology and the culture of surveillance.* New York University Press.

Haggerty, K. D., & Ericson, R. V. (2000). The surveillant assemblage. *British Journal of Sociology, 51*(4), 605–622. https://doi.org/10.1080/00071310020015280

Kostyuk, N., Chen, W., Das, V., Liang, F., & Hussain, M. M. (2017). *High-tech governance through big data surveillance: Tracing the global deployment of mass surveillance infrastructures, 1995 to present* (pp. 1–39). https://papers.ssrn.com/sol3/ papers.cfm?abstract_id=3030347

Liang, F. (2020). COVID-19 and health code: How digital platforms tackle the pandemic in China. *Social Media+ Society, 6*(3), 1–4. https://doi.org/10.1177/2056305120947657

Liang, F., Chen, Y., & Zhao, F. (2021). The platformization of propaganda: How Xuexi Qiangguo expands persuasion and assesses citizens in China. *International Journal of Communication,* 1855–1874.

Lips, A. M. B., Taylor, J. A., & Organ, J. (2009). Identity management, administrative sorting and citizenship in new modes of government. *Information, Communication & Society, 12*(5), 715–734. https://doi.org/10.1080/13691180802549508

16   *Fan Liang and Leiyuan Tian*

7
Lyon, D. (2007). *Surveillance studies: An overview.* Wiley.

Lyon, D. (2015). *Surveillance after Snowden.* John Wiley & Sons.

Marx, G. T. (2016). *Windows into the soul: Surveillance and society in an age of high technology.* University of Chicago Press.

Miller, J.A., & Miller, R. (1987). Jeremy Bentham's panoptic device. *October, 41,* 3–29. https://doi.org/10.2307/778327

Moss, W. W. (1996). Dang'an: Contemporary Chinese archives. *The China Quarterly, 145,* 112–129. https://doi.org/10.1017/S0305741000044155

Mosse, B., & Whitley, E. A. (2009). Critically classifying: UK e-government website benchmarking and the recasting of the citizen as customer. *Information Systems Journal, 19*(2), 149–173. https://doi.org/10.1111/j.1365-2575.2008.00299.x

Starr, P. (1992). Social categories and claims in the liberal state. *Social Research,* 263–295.

Taylor, J., Lips, M., & Organ, J. (2007). Information-intensive government and the layering and sorting of citizenship. *Public Money & Management, 27*(2), 161–164. https://doi.org/10.1111/j.1467-9302.2007.00573.x.

Van Dijck, J. (2014). Datafication, dataism and dataveillance: Big data between scientific paradigm and ideology. *Surveillance & Society, 12*(2), 197–208. https://doi.org/10.24908/ss.v12i2.4776

van Dijck, J., & Jacobs, B. (2019). Electronic identity services as sociotechnical and political-economic constructs. *New Media & Society,* 1–19. https://doi.org/10.1177/1461444819872537

Wood, D. M., Ball, K., Lyon, D., Norris, C., & Raab, C. (2006). *A report on the surveillance society* (pp. 1–98). Surveillance Studies Network.

Zhang, W. (2004). Dang an: A brief history of the Chinese imperial archives and its administration. *Journal of Archival Organization, 2*(1–2), 17–38. https://doi.org/10.1300/J201v02n01_03

Zuboff, S. (2019). *The age of surveillance capitalism: The fight for a human future at the new frontier of power.* Public Affairs.

2 The TikTok-ification of Chinese Society

Yi Guo

Digital Civilization: China's Ongoing Enterprise

On September 26, 2021, an international conference on the theme of "Towards a New Era of Digital Civilisation—Building a Community with a Shared Future in Cyberspace" was held in Wuzhen to discuss the digital possibilities of humankind. With more than 2,000 delegates from 96 countries and regions attending the conference, Chinese president Xi Jinping was physically absent from the conference venue and instead forwarded a congratulatory letter to be read out to the conference on his behalf. Despite the low-tech form of this gesture, his letter stated that given the pandemic situation and the profound changes in the world, "China is willing to work with other countries to shoulder the historical responsibility of promoting human progress by stimulating the digital economy vitality, enhancing the digital government efficiency, optimizing the digital social environment, setting up a digital cooperation structure, and building a strong digital security shield." These elements constitute what he terms in the letter as *digital civilization* (Xinhua News Agency, 26 September 2021).

Civilization is a buzzword that can be used for diverse pragmatic reasons. As Majid Tehranian (2004) has noted, the concept can simply mean "certain types of society" or alternatively be employed by politicians as "an ideological tool" to "legitimate certain hegemonic policies." If seen as an ideological tool, the concept of digital civilization parallels Xi's earlier domestic call for a *shuzi zhongguo* (digital China). In official discourse, the concept of digital China is often associated with advocacy for *wangluo qiangguo*, which has the dual meaning of "a powerful country in terms of internet development" and "strengthening the country through the internet." The construction of a "digital China," according to various official documents, involves three key areas: digital economy, digitized government services (or digital governance) and cyber security. Relevant measures include building new digital infrastructure (and especially to "strengthen key advances in critical and core technologies," as the party-state has proposed on numerous occasions), promoting the digital economy and supporting digital industries, employing digital technologies to

DOI: 10.4324/9781003299899-2

facilitate the modernization of the country's governing systems and capabilities, and enhancing governance and control to protect cyberspace security. If we compare these key areas and the measures taken to construct digital China with the Xi's proposal of digital civilization, it is safe to say that the call for a "digital civilization" appears to be encouraging an exportation of the mode of "digital China." Therefore, to understand the proposed "digital civilization" that China can bring to the world, we must interrogate the idea of digital China first.

The digitization of Chinese society (and particularly the development of digital technology and the digital economy) has long been of concern to Xi, as he emphasized at a Politburo meeting on October 18, 2021. Back in the 2000s, when he was working in the southern Chinese provinces of Fujian and Zhejiang, Xi had already proposed the concepts of "digital Fujian" and "digital Zhejiang," which can be seen as blueprints of the national strategy of "digital China" today (Xi, 2022). However, the idea behind these concepts was not novel at that time; instead, they were simply local implementations of a prevalent idea that was shared by the political elites of the Communist party back in the 1990s. As an active response to the global information optimism which began to be pervasive from the late 20th century, the leadership of China began to prioritize the informatization of the national economy and governance, aspiring "to marry the opportunities and dynamics of the global communication revolution with the country's unfinished process of industrialisation" (Dai, 2003). Invoking the discourse of *xinxi gaosu gonglu* (information highway), the central government under the leadership of Jiang Zemin had invested much to quickly construct a national grid of fiber-optic cables in aiming to surpass its American counterpart. At the local level, "digitisation of the city" was also enshrined in the policies of major cities. Apart from "digital Fujian" and "digital Zhejiang," there were also concepts such as "digital Hainan," "digital Shanxi," and "digital Shaanxi" during the same period (Wu, 2004, p. 300). As Western observers at the time pointed out, the Chinese pursuit of the information highway and digitization of society was based on the belief that "a developmental 'leapfrog can be achieved on the back of ICTs'." This belief and its practices, as they argued, were reminiscent of the hopes of the Great Leap Forward in the 1950s (Hughes & Wacker, 2003).

China's call for a digital civilization seems to echo this scenario of thirty years ago. Yet this time the call for a digital civilization is sufficiently backed by China's ongoing endeavor of supporting digital technologies and relevant infrastructures over the intervening decades. According to an official report (Cyberspace Administration of China, 2022) released publicly by the Cyberspace Administration of China, the country has established 1.425 million 5G base stations with a total of 355 million users by the end of 2021. One hundred percent of rural areas, including economically underdeveloped villages, have internet coverage. The construction of digital infrastructure, together with a mass of 1.032 billion internet users (or *netizens*), has facilitated a digital economic empire which is worth an estimated 7.1 trillion US dollars. As announced in the report, China "has set up the world's largest network infrastructure with advanced technology" and "leads the global digital economy." China has also established the National Integrated Online Government Service Platform to facilitate its digital governance. According to the report, more than 1 billion Chinese citizens are registered with the platform under their real names, which accounts for 71.4 percent of China's total population. The highly prosperous smartphone industry has further reinforced people's reliance on the internet. According to recent statistics, with China being the largest smartphone market in the world, there were more than 1.85 billion smartphones registered with telecommunication operators, plus approximately 6 billion phones being disposed of, by the end of 2021. With smartphones seeming to have become the number one indispensable possession for most Chinese people, many have adapted to accessing the internet primarily via their smartphone. As a consequence, there are social media platforms and smartphone super-apps that have become "an integral part of daily life" (Wei, 2021, January 20).

The internet has indeed been transforming the daily habits of many. In China today, there are few people who purchase clothes from department stores and pay by cash, and even domestic couples living in a same room can tend to communicate via WeChat or Tencent QQ text messages. Furthermore, the COVID-19 pandemic has not only made QR code systems indispensable but also made online forms of education, medical consulting, museum curation and shopping more prevalent than before. Neighbors who live in the same residential complex but were previously unfamiliar with each other are now gathering in the same WeChat group-chats, and the formerly "invisible" social organizers, as the ones who release notices in the group-chats, become more visible and powerful under the new name of *wanggeyuan* (community network workers). As the state media Xinhua News Agency (September 27, 2021) claimed in an article published after Xi's speech on digital civilization, "the development of internet in China has arrived at a new era of all-round penetration and cross-border convergence."

The digital developments mentioned here appear to set the national strategy of China's digital civilization efforts in a promising light. At the same time, they show that Chinese people have already been living increasingly digital lives before the term "digital civilization" was formally coined. Therefore, China's "digital civilization," whether it be a "certain type of society" or "an ideological tool," according to Majid Tehranian's dichotomy, is both a vision for the future and what has already been partially accomplished over the past decades. If we see China's digital civilization project as an unfinished but ongoing enterprise, what has already been accomplished at the current stage may help us imagine what the rest of it may bring about in the future.

Understanding Digital China Through Dominant Media

In the past few decades, digital China has garnered global attention. In the English-speaking world alone, there are numerous studies shedding light on the role that digital technologies have been playing in the formation of China's digital economy, culture and new social relations (e.g., Yang, 2009; Negro, 2017; Hong, 2017). Some even envisioned the development of the internet as "the latest catalyst for the strengthening of civil society in China" (Tai, 2006, p. 287). However, in contrast to the early generation of observers who conceived digital technologies as a promising instrument to empower grassroots citizens politically and thereby democratize mainland China, the findings of recent studies are not as optimistic as their predecessors. This parallels the global intellectual trend of rethinking the "delusion" of digital technologies and of the internet in particular. In recent years, media scholars have demonstrated that intensity of internet infrastructure and pervasiveness of internet access do not automatically guarantee a global understanding, a transformation of the economy, a renaissance of journalism or the empowerment of a democratic society (Curran et al., 2012).

In the Chinese context, empirical data has evidenced that well-developed internet communication technology has not inherently led to "ICT utilization for [political] participation in public affairs" (Wang, 2015). At the regional level, areas of higher internet penetration have not shown a higher level of public engagement when compared with areas of a lower internet penetration. Indeed, the local political culture in different Chinese regions matters more than new media technology in terms of promoting civic engagement (Zhou, 2015). Florian Schneider observes that, since the government adopts a "paternalistic approach to information and communication management," not all people are empowered equally by the internet. What is more, the internet, instead of facilitating contentions, has provided the Chinese authorities with more efficient authoritarian methods with which to govern digital China. The government directly manipulates and controls online discussions of sensitive topics while leaving space for negotiation of unimportant and apolitical issues. Online political discourses in Chinese cyberspace are organized around limited "recurring themes," and the appropriate public engagement becomes a way of legitimating and strengthening the party's control over digital China (Schneider, 2018, pp. 195–225).

The low quality of digital discourse is also at issue. David Herold finds the nature of Chinese online lives to be fairly apolitical, with the majority going online just for "cheap entertainment" (Herold, 2015). This is certainly not unique to Chinese society, and his finding echoes that of scholars such as James Curran, who points out that in the global context, social media is less about collective emancipation and social transformation than individual expressions for entertainment and leisure (Curran et al., 2012). Shouzhi Xia further demonstrates that entertainment media, in turn, acts as an instrument of "soft autocracy" that undermines audiences' critical abilities, thereby contributing to regime stability (Xia, 2021). Recent studies on Chinese online discourse also suggest that, unlike the European "public sphere" as envisioned by Habermas, online engagements among Chinese netizens can tend to be fairly "irrational" (Xie et al., 2021). As Rongbin Han (2018, pp. 21, 178) puts it, the internet "has done little to cultivate a pro-democracy discourse that spreads democratic values and ideas or even to mobilize netizens to struggle for a democratic regime," because "the pluralization of online expression has ironically contributed to authoritarian resilience."

This chapter conceptualizes "digital civilization" as a state of being. It deviates from the above literature by anthropologically reviewing and comparing the civilization with its dominant media in an effort to understand the former through the later. The French sociologist Emile Durkheim is perhaps among the early generation of scholars who are interested in this approach. He maintained, in a text published in 1901, that technologies of human societies are social products which "are always symptomatic of a determined state of civilisation, such that there are well-defined relations between them and the nature of the society that employs them" (Durkheim, 2006 [1901]). The Canadian historian Harold Innis (1949) further explicated the similarities and relationships between civilizations (including Chinese civilization) and their dominant media. For Innis, the media and its "bias of communication" shape the ethos of a civilization by providing a framework within which knowledge is disseminated, transmitted and interpreted. Here, the *media*, as Edward Comor (2001) adds, refers broadly to institutions, organizations and technologies. The biases of the dominant media then facilitate "the way of organizing society" and "common sense ways of thinking" (Comor, 2018). In the following sections, I will adopt an observational approach to investigating the similarity between the features of Chinese TikTok (Douyin) and new characteristics of the whole media culture as well as Chinese society today. I argue that as the digital enterprise grows within the Chinese sociopolitical context, the media culture and the lifestyle of Chinese people are becoming increasingly reflective of the nature and features of this currently all-pervasive social media application. This phenomenon, as an indicator of the unfinished but ongoing enterprise of digital civilization, may help us imagine what the remainder of the process may mean for China and the world.

TikTok in China: Its Shape and Features

TikTok, or *Douyin* in Chinese, has become a global phenomenon. It was originally designed in 2016 by a Beijing-based young tech company called Byte-Dance as a social media platform that enabled young adults to generate and share lip-sync music videos. Given its narrow audience and limited functions, the app was not received well initially. However, after ByteDance bought the Shanghai-based short-video platform Musical.ly and incorporated its basic features into ByteDance's signature algorithmic recommendation mechanism, a new edition of TikTok was born and thereafter attracted billions of users worldwide. As *The Economist* (2022, July 9) observes, TikTok spent only half the time that Facebook, YouTube and Instagram did in garnering over a billion users. It "has broken into the top tier of [the] global social media" club dominated by American tech giants. From 2020 to the first quarter of 2022, despite enduring suspicions voiced by some Western politicians, TikTok remained the most downloaded app in the world.

TikTok resembles an online audio-visual journal, in which people were encouraged to record and share their daily experiences by creating short videos each with a length of no more than 15 seconds. Despite the limited genres of content in its early days, TikTok now hosts short videos spanning a wide range of genres such as entertainment, pranks, visual tricks, jokes, physical stunts and edited news items. Over the past couple of years, celebrity endorsements along with the app's algorithmic recommendations, personalized and engaging content, successful marketing strategies and user-friendly interface have made it the most popular short-video platform in China (Kovács, 2022). According to a briefing released by ByteDance in 2020, at that time more than 600 million Chinese users actively accessed TikTok every day, accounting for half of China's total population (Li, 2020, September 17). A more recent survey also revealed that, compared with the situation in the United States, Chinese users spent more time on TikTok; more than half of Chinese respondents spent one or more hours on TikTok per day (Yang, 2022). This is particularly notable considering that Chinese people's average time available for leisure is only 3.8 hours per day according to statistics in 2021 (Li, 2021, October 11). If living in China, it is fairly common to see people watching TikTok videos at any time in public. It is not uncommon to hear the signature sound effects of the app ringing out incongruently in hospitals, libraries, train carriages, aircraft cabins and many other venues that were previously expected to be relatively quiet.

It is also notable that, although they do share some similarities (such as logo, interface, functionality and business mode), the Chinese version of TikTok is different from its international twin in terms of users/audience and content. The Chinese TikTok targets a wider range of audiences and thus exerts greater influence on Chinese society. In contrast to the overseas version of TikTok that mainly targets Generation Z, its twin in China is particularly popular among people aged in their fifties and sixties partly as a result of early retirement.[1] TikTok also launched initiatives in 2021 to further boost its number of older users. In many cases, the app has become the most essential media outlet that senior people access in order to know about the outside world. While in the United States most TikTok users live in urban areas, with the deep penetration of mobile internet and TikTok in China's rural areas, users from small suburbs and villages have become a critical portion of the app's Chinese audience. In recent years TikTok has also been trying to help boost the referral traffic of TikTokers producing short videos on the topics of *san'nong* (i.e., rural areas, farmers, and agriculture). However, the users/ audience often have low education and lack proper media literacy due to the particular and painful historical roots of Chinese education (see, Wang & Lo, 2018), which can tend to impact upon the level of analysis and accuracy in the way issues are presented.

The content produced is also a prominent aspect of differences between the Chinese and international versions of the app. The operation team of TikTok's international version has publicly claimed that it does not censor content critical of China. Yet the domestic version is never evasive regarding its strict approach to censorship. According to its CEO, by April of 2018 Chinese Tik-Tok employed a team of over 1,500 people charged with censoring its online content, with that team enlarging "every day" (Liu, 2018, April 19). On its official website, ByteDance keeps recruiting Content Censorship Coordinators "responsible for monitoring and censoring online content including pictures, texts, videos, and livestreams." It is also easy to distinguish the unique tone of Chinese TikTok, which I will explore later.

Positive Energy

TikTok particularly welcomes short videos deemed to be of "positive energy," and the Party-state's involvement in their production and dissemination has also been uncovered (Litzinger & Ni, 2021; Chen et al., 2020). Coined ten years ago, the term "positive energy" (or *zhengnengliang* in Chinese) refers to an ideology that prefers cheerful, optimistic, patriotic discourses aligned in favor of the Party-state. The Chinese authorities see the promotion of positive narratives as an efficient way of maintaining the legitimacy of the Party-state and thus encourage these as being "mainstream" and "healthy." In recent years, the preference for "positive" content has further combined with a Chinese misinterpretation of the Western concept of *constructive journalism*. The media, be it legacy or digital, are tasked with disseminating "positive" content that is "constructive" in propagating the Party's indoctrination and securing the stability of the regime. Consequently, thousands of legacy media outlets and government agencies have opened accounts to create and share "positive" videos on TikTok. These videos, often highly staged, emotional, affective, heart-warming and with the privilege of being longer than 15 seconds, will be given more chance of curation by TikTok's esoteric algorithm. These seemingly well-received videos released by parties of an official background have also inspired numerous online celebrities and influencers to integrate similar positive elements into their own videos in an effort to garner traffic (*liuliang*). Today, positive-energy videos have become dominant on the Chinese TikTok, as highlighted in its 2021 report. According to the revealed data, in 2021 alone, the number of uploaded videos shedding light on topics of "reunion," "starting a relationship," "getting married" and "persistence" transcended those of videos talking about "farewell," "breaking up," "divorce" and "giving up" by 10.71 million, 15.55 million, 16.24 million and 39.21 million, respectively. Positive topics always triumphed over their opposites.

Cyber Patriotism/Nationalism

On Chinese TikTok, positive energy often combines with state-sponsored patriotism and even cyber-nationalism. Most patriotic videos are addressed in a direct way. It is common to see short videos with passionate background music narrating or exaggerating Chinese achievements. These video clips also insert patriotic phrases such as "China is the big winner (*zhongguo shi zuida yingjia*)," "My country is great (*lihai le wode guo*)," "China's good luck is coming (*guoyun laile*)" and "I feel extremely happy as I was born in China (*shengzai zhongguo beigan xingfu*)" as conspicuous banners or captions to assert a patriotic tone. In video clips showing China's reactions in the diplomatic arena, chauvinist captions and banners such as "[China] imperiously responds (*baqi huiying*)" and "China sends the most assertive warnings (*zhongguo fachu zuiqiang jinggao*)" will be foregrounded to emphasize China's powerful diplomacy. There are also many videos glorifying or flattering Chinese or pro-Chinese politicians with highly complementary terms and exaggerations (Florian, 2022, May 15).

Defiling China's competitors or "enemies" is another technique used to express feelings of patriotism and nationalism. This includes inserting sensational banners or captions such as "America [or any other Western country] is screwed [or freaked out]," vilifying or mocking foreign nationals and using intimidating words or hate speech. After the speaker of the US House of Representatives Nancy Pelosi wrapped up her quick visit to Taiwan in August 2022, a video uploaded by the state media outlet *People's Daily* became quickly popular on Chinese TikTok. With over 1.62 million "thumbs-up," the video vilified Pelosi by caricaturing her as a witch riding on a broom. The caption beneath read, "Pelosi left Taiwan amid swearing." The caption was not telling a lie. After Pelosi announced her plan to visit Taiwan, and particularly when her plane was crossing the Taiwan strait, thousands of Chinese TikTokers posted videos calling Pelosi "the old witch," and the comment areas were full of swear words directed against the Congresswoman. A few videos also showed TikTokers training toy guns on their own smartphones' screen, on which was a map following the coordinate of Pelosi's plane. Others grafted the image of Pelosi's head onto versions of the arcade game Whac-A-Mole, advocating "beat the old witch to death."

Infantilized Amusement

The Pelosi scenario touched on here illustrates the phenomenon of so-called playful patriotism on Chinese TikTok. As scholars have shown, many TikTok videos adopt a "playful" approach to promoting patriotism or even cyber-nationalism (Chen et al., 2020). That is, the videos support the established Party-state discourse and legitimate the regime in ways that are seen as playful and amusing by their audience. In this regard Pelosi is not alone, because both the US President Joe Biden and his predecessor Donald Trump have also been derided on the app. Their embarrassing moments are edited into short videos as evidence of political incapability to amuse Chinese TikTokers, patriotic feelings being aroused through this amusement. There are also many nationalist videos making fun of people from poor countries in rather racist ways, playing on stereotypes to reassure their audience that other countries are not as good as China (Khatsenkova, 2022, August 1).

Entertainment is the most salient feature of TikTok. As a survey has shown, entertainment gratification is the primary reason most Chinese people use the app (Yang & Ha, 2021). Yet, as the Pelosi scenario shows, there are notable childish tendencies behind the amusement feature of Chinese TikTok. Particularly when it comes to complex issues, such as the Russia-Ukraine war or US-China tensions, many Chinese TikTokers tend to provide infantile interpretations by personifying the arena of international politics as a kid's playhouse. For example, a popular short video produced by the state's propaganda apparatus *China Daily* interprets Joe Biden's infrastructure plan to rival China's Belt and Road Initiative as "plagiarizing China's schoolwork." Numerous TikTokers, albeit lacking general political knowledge, present themselves as experts commenting on intricate international affairs with terms that would otherwise be used by children. Their opinions provide nothing but infantilized amusement that downgrades the complexity of politics. When Pelosi's plane was flying across on the Taiwan Strait on August 2, 2022, in support of China's assertive response, many patriotic TikTokers called for China's People Liberation Army (PLA) to "bomb her plane." Yet upon the plane safely landing in Taipei without the PLA's military intervention, the TikTokers frantically shifted their rhetoric in order to legitimate the reason why the PLA did not bomb Pelosi's plane as follows:

> Your mom does not like your bad classmate and has repeatedly asked you not to bring him your home. Yet you defied her by taking him to your home when your mom is not outside. Will your mom immediately beat the classmate in front of you? Obviously not. She will only beat you when the guy is gone.

This infantilized narrative equates the tensions between the PLA, Taipei and Pelosi to some kind of morbid family sitcom, providing little insight into the complexity of the situation.

The infantilization and political immaturity of Chinese TikTok parallel the situation of the general Chinese online population. According to the China Internet Network Information Centre (CINIC), less than 10 percent of

Chinese netizens have attended tertiary education whereas the majority have only graduated from primary school or junior high school. As for occupational status, students, freelancers, migrant workers, labor force workers, and retired and unemployed people account for 67.8 percent, with 85.2 percent of Chinese netizens earning less than the national average income.

Valueless Information

It might be expected that when those from underrepresented communities in the real world become TikTokers in the virtual world this would provide a valuable increase in information about and visibility of their situation to broader society. However, it feels safe to argue that TikTok has instead produced a greater amount of valueless information. "Record your wonderful life," the slogan of Chinese TikTok goes. Yet it seems that often TikTokers do not have much to say apart from jokes and pranks. If you search for the term "Stew myself in an iron wok," more than a thousand hits show TikTokers sitting in woks and basting themselves! There are also numerous mundane videos showing TikTokers eating meals, sleeping, playing online games and showing-off wealth, yet these seemingly tedious videos are surprisingly received well. One of the limited contributions to public life might be the endless invention of neologisms that do not really connote new ideas. Despite the concerns of serious linguists (Chen et al., 2022), trending neologisms are often borrowed by legacy media and become rampant in news items. The official accounts of legacy media and government agencies do upload videos that are useful and pertinent to public life. Yet at the same time they also post staged and appropriated positive-energy videos with self-purchased traffic and solicited positive comments from their own staff members.

Information is particularly valueless for the public good if inaccurate or fabricated. I am not primarily talking about misinformation underpinning conspiracy theories nor about weaponized disinformation used in digital warfare, since these are fairly common around the world and remain an unresolved issue globally. Here I am more concerned about intentionally inaccurate or fabricated information that has significant influence on people's intellectual life. Despite TikTok's stated efforts at regulating fake news, it is the case that pseudo-surveys, pseudo-science and distorted history are still very common. Chinese TikTok empowers people who may not have adequate knowledge about an issue to nevertheless present themselves as experts. In these videos, no context is provided for the pseudo-science, no source is given for the distorted history and no rigorous methodology is presented for the pseudo-surveys. The pseudo-experts simply show fabricated arguments without proper evidence, and the arguments are usually false. These videos, instead of doing good to the public life, only act to undermine human intelligence by providing valueless pseudo-knowledge to an audience that does not demand higher proof.

Templates and Duplication

TikTok has developed an auxiliary application called *Jianying* (CapCut) to enable TikTokers to make short videos in minutes. *Jianying* as a handy video editing tool provides loads of ready-to-use templates, background music, sound effects, stickers and camera filters. If a video becomes popular on TikTok, users can easily make a similar one by mechanically applying the same templates and sounds with just one click. TikTok with the help of *Jianying*, therefore, becomes a standardized product line that manufactures cookie-cutter videos. The extensive duplications are not only restricted to the art design of videos but also entail genres, stories, dubbing and narratives. As a result, positive energy, cyber patriotism and nationalism, infantilization and even valueless information are growing exponentially on Chinese Tik-Tok. Amid complaints about life and conditions in the Wuhan cabin hospitals, numerous positive-energy videos depicted medical workers and patients dancing to background music of popular Chinese songs. These videos are strikingly similar in narratives, camera shots and style of editing (Zheng, 2020, February 11). Another positive-energy scenario is the viral trend of posting videos singing and dancing to "Listen to Me Say Thank You" for medical workers when going to undertake a COVID test in public during 2022 (Zuo, 2022, March 10). These highly staged and duplicated videos promoting people's gratitude toward healthcare workers and the benevolence of government cadres actually aroused some backlash online as they reminded people of the notorious "gratitude education campaign" that had been mounted during the initial stages of the COVID-19 outbreak (Mai, 2020, October 10). Cyber patriotism/nationalism, combined with a sense of infantilization, is also undoubtedly duplicated in bulk. When a prototype TikTok video entitled "The imperious oaths throughout Chinese dynasties" became popular in May 2021, thousands of imitations appeared. In these videos, the storylines and content are exactly the same—a group of Chinese students reading patriotic sentences in turn. The student protagonists, though not the same group as the original video, repeat the same patriotic words such as "Those who offend us Chinese will be eliminated no matter how far away they are" and do so with a similarly aggressive tone and look (Yang, 2022). Among the enthusiastic and fanatical comments on these duplicated videos, few had pointed out that most of the patriotic and chauvinist sentences were not really "oaths" used in Chinese history but rather lyrics or lines from contemporary TV dramas. Similar scenarios appear very common on Chinese TikTok.

The TikTok-ification of Chinese Media Culture

TikTok has been affecting the entire mass media culture over the past few years. People living in China will have no difficulty in finding that both legacy and digital media outlets are becoming TikTok-like in terms of function, tone and content. Echoing what is happening on TikTok, positive energy, cyber patriotism and nationalism, amusement and infantilization, and valueless and fabricated information or misinformation are intertwined and duplicated in this converging media sphere.

For a long time in China there was a clear demarcation between legacy media (such as newspapers, television and radio) and digital platforms. Legacy media had been seen as the "mainstream" media by Chinese authorities. "Mainstream (*zhuliu*)," in the Chinese context, is not used to describe the popularity of the media but rather to highlight their intimacy with the government. Historically designed as propaganda apparatuses of the Party-state, legacy media share many similarities with government agencies. For example, within the party bureaucracy the Editor-in-Chief of the state media Xinhua News Agency equates to the Minister of Education, and the Head of China Central Television (CCTV) equates to the Deputy Secretary of Defense. Despite investigative journalists sometimes pushing for democratic reforms by scrutinizing misbehaviors of the government in the heyday of economic reform back in the 1990s and 2000s (Wang, 2016; Zhao, 1998), legacy media consistently shared a similarly serious discourse feature with their government counterparts in contrast to that of digital media. However, the demarcation of discourse features between the two has gradually become less clear. As a reaction to the triumph of digital media and alternative voices, in addition to the taming and repression of critical journalism (Tong, 2019; Svensson, 2017; Repnikova, 2017, pp. 206–221), the Chinese authorities in recent years have called for the transformation of a *xinxing zhuliu meiti* (new mainstream media) to reinforce the capabilities of the Party's mouthpieces in the "ideological battlefront." The new mainstream media, as the Party envisions, are still partisan but adopt trendy technologies and features of digital media to appeal to the tastes of audiences in the digital age. Consequently, numerous legacy media conglomerates have established new divisions and recruited young talent in order to develop their digital enterprises.

For the new mainstream media, a notable strategy is to work with TikTok to extend their reach of influence. By the end of 2018 a total of 1,344 state media outlets had opened accounts on TikTok, and the number will be much higher today. Over the past two years I have talked to nearly a hundred people making and uploading TikTok videos on behalf of diverse legacy media outlets, many of them referring to a new golden creed: "Be TikTok if you want traffic." In this light, it is fairly common to find news announcers of CCTV, who were previously seen as serious mouthpieces of the Party-state, performing mini talk shows on TikTok using trendy internet language. What is more, many legacy media outlets have gone to great lengths to "be TikTok" even on content released outside of the application. This not only results from the inertia of working with TikTok but is also their tactic for dealing with the global trend toward accelerated information production (Lash, 2002, pp. 150–151; Rauch, 2018, pp. 2–8) and the increasingly restrictive media environment in China. For them, "being TikTok" is easy, safe and lucrative. Therefore, the declining of quality journalism is increasingly being substituted by what I would call a "TikTok-ified" journalism.

Scenarios on TikTok, then, are extended to the discursive sphere of legacy media. For example, CCTV's signature news program *Xinwen Lianbo* (News Bulletin), reminiscent of the time before China's economic reform, every evening now restricts its topics to either China's achievements or the chaos of foreign countries. Like many other media outlets, it spares no effort in criticizing the United States and other "hostile forces." Over a period of more than two years the program continuously reported on the rising COVID cases in America to demonstrate that the American government was incapable of handling the pandemic. Compared with the scenario of 20 years ago, investigative journalism and lifestyle journalism are both retreating from newspapers. Instead, a more sensational and TikTok-ified popular journalism that "places a much greater emphasis on infotainment" and that uses the patriotic and infantile language of TikTok is rising (Wang et al., 2018; Xin, 2018). Many pundits, scholars and media professionals confound the Western "constructive journalism" with the outdated concept of "development journalism" and loudly argue that critical journalism revealing the dark side of a situation does no good to the progress of Chinese society. Consequently, heart-warming and inspirational stories narrating "good people doing good things (*haoren haoshi*)" become dominant. Applying "templates" to the duplication of (mis) information also becomes a common media-scape. As Western observers have found, it is common for Chinese newspapers to use identical front pages for their coverage (Yan, 2018, September 3). Similarly, when a television show gets popular, numerous copycats quickly appear. In many cases, the prototype and the copycats share the same production team and guests. The positive news stories in legacy media are becoming identical too. When the COVID-19 outbreak swept Wuhan in 2020, thousands of news stories from diverse Chinese cities separately reported individuals in their city donating money to Wuhan. However, all of these reports used the same sentence to narrate their identical stories: "[The anonymous individual] left ten thousand Chinese Yuan at the police station and ran out." Readers cannot help but wonder at so many individuals from diverse cities supposedly having "left" an identical amount of money at an identical place (the police station) and then identically "running out" after doing so.

Social media platforms are also becoming TikTok-ified. The transformation of the microblogging service Weibo is a typical example. Once seen as the Chinese equivalent to Twitter and a catalyst for social reforms in the 2000s, Weibo today has lost its potential as a public sphere to facilitate deliberative democracy in the Habermasian sense. As scholars argue, it has in recent years "transformed from an online space for public discussions to a platform for marketing and advertising, and entertainment uses" (Jia & Han, 2022). Apart from the infantilized amusement and valueless information that undermine critical thinking and squeeze out the discursive space of dissent, the sentiments of patriotism, nationalism and anti-democracy, as well as fake news, hate speech and distorted histories that facilitate political immaturity and anti-intellectualism, are becoming more pervasive than those of ten years ago (Zhang et al., 2018; Lu, 2020; Yang & Fang, 2021).

A Digital Civilization or A TikTok-ified Society?

Over the past ten years China has certainly benefitted from the process of the developing digital economy (Ma et al., 2021, pp. 13–26). Yet when the popularity of digital technologies has combined with China's unique political culture, society as a whole can be seen to be becoming TikTok-ified in the process.

TikTok monitors you and analyzes your preferences when you use it, which helps optimize its algorithmic recommendations. Similarly, people are increasingly being watched in digital China; someone knows them better than they know themselves. As Western observers have noticed, surveillance cameras with facial and voice recognition functions are growing fast in Chinese localities over the past ten years, making China "the world's largest surveillance system" (Mcgregor, 2020, November 3). A sense of mystery and insecurity may arise given the fact that people still do not know what the pervasive cameras are used for. The COVID-19 pandemic has further legitimized the widespread use of surveillance technologies in the name of buttressing happiness for all. In a northeast city of China, the local government proudly announced that a surveillance system called "Cloud-eye" had been installed in the local cabin facility for isolating patients affected the coronavirus. The government explained to the public that once a patient tries to walk out from his cell the artificial intelligence camera will automatically recognize who he is and send an alarm to the warden immediately. This would also trigger a warning, asking the patient to go back to his cell. In this case, the formerly clandestine behavior of the surveillance system has become overt, and the furtive panopticon is transformed into a public good. Digital technologies are also utilized to monitor what people think. In July of 2022, a research institute with an official background proudly showcased their latest surveillance invention—a "mind-reading" AI machine that could help distinguish whether or not the Party's indoctrination has been well received by an individual. The news was quickly wiped from Chinese social media after it aroused a public backlash (Towey, 2022, July 11). The ubiquity of surveillance in many cases could be argued to not bring "happiness for all" but rather produce a repressive culture. For example, the word-processing software WPS, the Chinese equivalent of Microsoft Word, was accused of clandestinely accessing users' documents and deleting "improper content" from them (Liu & Murphy, 2022, July 16). In China's southeast city of Dongguan a surveillance technique called Rental Housing Management, which was deployed to monitor rural migrants, allegedly "creates difficulties with migrants' social interaction and community building" as a by-product of its system of observation (Gong, 2016). At universities, young students' action of *jubao* (i.e., secretly recording and reporting teachers for politically incorrect speech) may result in a chill effect among academics and self-censorship in classes (Hessler, 2022, May 16).

Similar to TikTok, digital China more broadly is also full of valueless efforts. In 2021, the term *neijuan* (involution) became one of the top ten buzzwords in China. It refers to repeated but valueless effort that does not result in productivity. As one of China's propaganda apparatuses CGTN admits, with the structural change of Chinese society, infinite overtime and extra effort are becoming difficult to find resulting in a better life for people but instead produce "a prevalent sense of being stuck in an ever so draining rat race where everyone loses" (Zhou, 2020, December 4). The duplication of positive energy then becomes a pacifier to relieve people's anxiety over *neijuan*. Apart from the excessive positive information produced (or fabricated) by the media, government agencies and social organizations at all levels have launched numerous activities and initiatives to encourage and praise people displaying positive energy. In these activities, people who work hard in a difficult situation will be granted the title of *haoren* (good man) and their stories will be publicized in order to educate others. These positive stories, as scholars demonstrate, produce "self-disciplined docile subjects, and quietly resolves the tension between mobilisation and control by having subjects internalise the interests of the state as their own good" (Chen & Wang, 2019). "You didn't live a good life because you didn't work hard" becomes a self-fulfilling prophecy that inveigles people into further repeated but valueless efforts regardless of whether the source of their problems may actually derive from social structures and institutions.

With the anxiety of *neijuan*, people living in this digital China are getting more used to inventing new terms. First, there is the rise of dispensable neologisms. They are dispensable because they, as with the many new terms produced by TikTok, provide no innovation but simply convey old ideas. For example, the newly coined term *ye jingji* (evening economy) is commonly used in the economic reports of local governments, but it in fact refers to a very old business activity—the night market. The new term *quanyu jingtai guanli* (all-region silent management) appears in local policies regarding containing COVID-19 yet is actually just another way of saying "lockdown." Second, government and industry both appear powerless to resist the allure of trendy tech buzzwords that arise, tending toward overuse to the point of rendering the terms meaningless. In China today, for example, the term "Metaverse" has been associated with nearly everything regardless of the half-baked understanding most have of it. Over the past year there have been Metaverse toilets, Metaverse hotels and Metaverse restaurants, to name a few. Despite the hype, these Metaverse-things have no obvious difference from those without the word "Metaverse" attached and no clear connection to the virtual-reality concept for which it was coined. The proliferation and hype of new terms like these may perhaps indicate a societal anxiety to fill the vacuum of social progress in the context of the recent economic slowdown or to relieve social tensions in a post-pandemic China.

However, there are also buzzwords that have aroused public backlash. For example, *eyi fanxiang* (malicious returnee), denoting "anyone returning from a middle or high-risk region" during the COVID-19 pandemic, received wide denunciation immediately after it was coined (Zhang, 2021, January 21). Another example arose in the summer of 2022, when dozens of Chinese cities imported a Japanese mode of business promotion activity called Natsumatsuri to help boost their economies. Yet anti-Natsumatsuri events were held in many cities to call for boycotts due to a misunderstanding of the term. In Japan, Natsumatsuri (夏祭り) means "summer festival" and is a series of night market activities. However, whereas the word "祭り (*matsuri*)" literally means "festival" in Japanese, it means "worship (ji, 祭)" in Chinese, which triggered inaccurate associations. Many protesters claimed that Natsumatsuri is "traditional Japanese worship activities in summer" (an inaccuracy that was even included in the entry on Baike, the Chinese equivalent of Wikipedia) and that to organize such activities in China is not patriotic. Misinformation reinforced this misunderstanding. Some asserted that such "worship" had been used in Japanese history to bless Japan during its invasion in China. Some went further to assert that Japan had sponsored Chinese cities to organize such activities and that its real intention was to humiliate China. Natsumatsuri is neither a "traditional" nor a "worship" activity. As a purely business activity, it is also irrelevant to the unsettling history between China and Japan. However, these sophomoric interpretations, mixed with misinformation and nationalism, led to the cancellation of Natsumatsuri in most cities that had been planning to hold them.

The case of anti-Natsumatsuri events lead to another similarity between TikTok and the digital China of today—the combination of infantilization, valueless and misleading information, and sentiments of patriotism or nationalism. The Chinese psychologist Wu Zhihong recently released a book that included the argument that most Chinese people are psychologically "giant babies" and that contemporary China is a "nation of giant infants." Although the bestseller was banned in China, the word "giant babies" was honored among the top ten Chinese buzzwords in 2018 because many believe it perfectly describes a Chinese way of living today. Twenty years ago, Children's Day was only a public holiday celebrated among children. In this present time, adults often seem more excited than their children to be involved in the celebrations of the day. Moreover, childish expressions that were formerly only used between children are now commonly used by adults in their daily lives. For example, many adults at work call themselves *baobao* (babies) and their colleagues *xiao huoban* (little playmates). A more concerning issue is the infantilized way of thinking that permeates public life and international politics. For example, when a new wave of COVID-19 broke out in the coastal city Xiamen in August 2022, medical workers were seen swabbing the mouths of fish to test for the virus (Davidson, 2022, August 18). As the 2022 Russia-Ukraine war broke out, Chinese shoppers rushed to a Russia-accredited online store and bought up Russian snacks in support of Russia's invasion of Ukraine (Sun, 2022, May 5).

As with what occurs on TikTok, the ubiquity of misinformation is a catalyst for the infantilization of society. The issue is that a significant portion of misleading information disseminated in China is produced by mass media and high-profile pundits. In the early days of Chinese economic reform, experts were the ones leading the intellectual life of Chinese development. Yet in the new digital China, many pundits only care about generating "traffic" as if they are *wanghong* (internet celebrities). In recent years it has been not uncommon to hear experts providing misleading advice and recommendations designed to please ears rather than to educate—for example, some said that those who refuse to have babies in order to support society should be fined and punished, while others suggested that disposable surgical facemasks could be safely reused after being steamed in a pot at home. A nationally accredited medical expert advised that people should "take Chinese medicine as early as possible to prevent against the BA.5 strain of COVID-19." He also asked people to soak their used facemasks before disposing of them, which contradicted the recommendations of the World Health Organization. At a time when promotion of misleading information is discrediting the group of established specialists as a whole, pseudo-experts jump on stage to take advantage. In a digital age when "no expert need apply" (Nichols, 2017, p. 170), these tend to mainly disseminate misinformation, which leads to further infantilization, if not outright anti-intellectualism.

In late 2015, President Xi announced that "patriotism is the core of the national ethos." This was more expressing a clear expectation from the leadership rather than reflecting a homogeneous situation at the time. To meet his expectation, state-sponsored patriotism is now running high. In 2019 the central government released the Outline of New-Era Patriotic Education and launched campaigns for a thorough indoctrination of the Party's interpretation of patriotism. This state-sponsored patriotism seems to have been successful. According to a survey conducted by the state media outlet *China Youth Daily* in 2019, more than 94% of the respondents reported having experienced moments in which they were "overwhelmed with patriotic feelings (*aiguo xin baopeng*, 爱国心爆棚)" (Wang & Chen, 2019 September 26). Even though the Chinese authorities have never publically advocated nationalism per se, the state-sponsored patriotism is in practice developing toward a popular nationalism (Zeng & Sparks, 2019). This discourse of popular nationalism is, like TikTok, expressed through common templates. These discursive templates include "China is destined to be great and the hostile countries are destined to get weaker," "If you don't think China is great or if you think other countries are great, then you are a traitor," "You should not criticize China, because other countries are doing worse" and "You should not criticize China and if you do, you are a poodle of the hostile countries," to name a few. One can easily observe the pervasiveness of these templates and their impact by revisiting the popular discourses surrounding recent events involving the United States, Australia, India, and Japan.

However, popular nationalism does not only remain at the discursive level. On August 10, 2022, a young Chinese woman was detained in public for wearing a Japanese traditional kimono in a Japan-themed business area of Suzhou in China's east. According to a leaked video clip, the police officer told the girl, "if you wear Chinese traditional costume *hanfu*, it's okay, but you are wearing a kimono and you are a Chinese." Perhaps more shocking was that many netizens supported the policeman's obviously illegal behavior and abused the poor girl online with curse words (Davidson, 2022, August 16). This, like the anti-Natsumatsuri activities, is a bad sign illustrating how aggressive popular nationalism can become in a sophomoric and infantilized context.

Conclusion

Scientists posit that an entwined future between media and human society is becoming more likely (Lee, 2020). This chapter has provided a vivid case from China where the media landscape and the lifestyle of Chinese society are becoming TikTok-ified. Mirroring the nature of content currently most popular on Chinese TikTok, surveillance, infantilization, fabrication, duplicated and valueless information, and state patriotism trending toward popular nationalism are more pervasive in public life in China than the situation ten years ago. If the popularity of TikTok is a totem representing the progress of China's ongoing enterprise of digitization, the TikTok-ification of the media culture and ways of living may reflect what an unfinished digital civilization looks like. The TikTok-ification of Chinese society constitutes a mechanism of "soft control," much like what TikTok employs with its audience to maintain its popularity and place in people's daily lives. The ubiquity of surveillance makes everyone "transparent" to the government and can create a repressive culture. Infantilization, mixed with a swarm of duplicated and valueless (mis) information, deprives people of critical thinking, undoes sophistication and produces an "illusion of knowledge" (Weber & Koehler, 2017). The hype of new buzzwords creates the sense of "vicarious progress" in the context of a sluggish economy. Positive energy distracts people from the anxiety of *nei-juan*, inducing them to put more effort into their work regardless of sociopolitical problems such as inequality. State patriotism and popular nationalism, often combined with infantilization and misinformation, provide occasions of catharsis while further chilling discourse from the more limited rational voices within society. These outcomes may not all be entirely projected by the authorities but would certainly be favored by authority.

Vincent Mosco (2004, pp. 10–43) reminds us of the cultural implication of the "digital sublime" beyond technological criticism and political economy. For him, the myths derived from digital optimism, although having turned out to be merely "seductive tales containing promises unfulfilled or even unfulfillable," have special meanings for human society. As Mosco demonstrates, cyberspace "does not mark the end of history (or even the start of a new age), does not presage the end of geography (place matters more than ever), nor does it signal the end of politics (the struggle for power goes on)," but rather the sustaining effort of voicing the "digital sublime" and its myths benefit experts of technology, internet companies, governments and media outlets. They never tire of manufacturing and promoting the myths of cyberspace because their "legitimacy today is based on identification with this future wave." This might similarly be the case for China's aspired exportation of the *digital civilization* concept. In this chapter, I do not imply that a digital civilization, as to what China envisions as its own or the world's future, is a necessarily negative thing. It is also clear that surveillance society, nationalism and infantilization are global issues rather than being the problem of a particular nation (Mathiesen, 2013, pp. 17–23; Cross, 2010; Bieber, 2018). Yet, as the chapter illustrates, people are often as willing to accept this described TikTok-ification of society as readily as they do TikTok itself, and many of us are as uncritical of such phenomenon within our own society as we are of the manipulation of the TikTok algorithm. This is perhaps the most concerning part of the issue and one that deserves scrutiny.

Note

1 Compared with the retirement ages in Australia, the United States and the United Kingdom, China has a low average retirement age of 54.

References

Bieber, F. (2018). Is nationalism on the rise? Assessing global trends. *Ethnopolitics*, *17*(5), 519–540.

Chen, M., Liu, S., & Zhang, S. (2022). Internet Language Study in China. In Z. Ye (Ed.), *The Palgrave Handbook of Chinese Language Studies* (pp. 275–296). Singapore: Palgrave Macmillan.

Chen, X., Kaye, D. B. V., & Zeng, J. (2020). #PositiveEnergy Douyin: Constructing 'playful patriotism' in a Chinese short-video application. *Chinese Journal of Communication*, *14*(1), 97–117.

Chen, Z., & Wang, C. Y. (2019). The discipline of happiness: The Foucauldian use of the 'positive energy' discourse in China's ideological works. *Journal of Current Chinese Affairs*, *48*(2), 201–225.

Comor, E. (2001). Harold Innis and 'the bias of communication. *Information, Communication & Society*, *4*(2), 272–294.

Comor, E. (2018). Ubiquitous media and monopolies of knowledge: The approach of Harold Innis. In M. S. Daubs & V. R. Manzerolle (Eds.), *Mobile and ubiquitous media: Critical and international perspectives* (pp. 183–200). Peter Lang.

Cross, G. (2010). *Men to boys: The making of modern immaturity*. Columbia University Press.

Curran, J., Freedman, D., & Fenton, N. (2012). Conclusion. In J. Curran, N. Fenton, & D. Freedman (Eds.), *Misunderstanding the internet* (pp. 179–185). Routledge.

Cyberspace Administration of China. (2022, August 2). Shuzi zhongguo fazhan baogao (2021) [Development of digital China: A report, 2021]. *CAC*. Retrieved August 2, 2022, from www.cac.gov.cn/2022-08/02/c_1661066515613920.htm

Dai, X. (2003). ICTs in China's development strategy. In C. R. Hughes & G. Wacker (Eds.), *China and the internet: Politics of the digital leap forward* (pp. 8–29). Routledge.

Davidson, H. (2022, August 18). City in China orders fish swabbed for Covid. *The Guardian*. www.theguardian.com/world/2022/aug/18/city-in-china-orders-fish-swabbed-for-covid

Durkheim, E. (2006 [1901]). Technology (1901). In N. Schlanger (Ed.), *Techniques, technology and civilisation* (pp. 31–32). Berghahn Books.

The Economist. (2022, July 9). The all-conquering quaver. *The Economist*. Retrieved September 10, 2022, from www.economist.com/interactive/briefing/2022/07/09/the-all-conquering-quaver

Florian, A. (2022, May 15). Chinese TikTok users are in love with 'Daddy Putin'. *Foreign Diplomacy*. Retrieved August 10, 2022, from https://foreignpolicy.com/2022/05/15/china-russia-putin-tiktok-douyin/

Gong, Y. R. (2016). Renting house management as surveillance of Chinese rural migrants: The case of hillside compound in Dongguan. *Housing Studies*, *31*(8), 998–1018.

Han, R. (2018). *Contesting cyberspace in China: Online expression and authoritarian resilience*. Columbia University Press.

Herold, D. K. (2015). Users, not netizens: Spaces and practices on the Chinese internet. In P. Marolt & D. K. Herold (Eds.), *China online: Locating society in online spaces* (pp. 20–30). Routledge.

Hessler, P. (2022, May 16). A teacher in China learns the limits of free expression. *The New Yorker*. www.newyorker.com/magazine/2022/05/16/a-teacher-in-china-learns-the-limits-of-free-expression

Hong, Y. (2017). *Networking China: The digital transformation of the Chinese economy*. University of Illinois Press.

Hughes, C. R., & Wacker, G. (2003). Introduction: China's digital leap forward. In C. R. Hughes & G. Wacker (Eds.), *China and the internet: Politics of the digital leap forward* (pp. 1–7). Routledge.

Innis, H. A. (1949). The bias of communication. *The Canadian Journal of Economics and Politics Science*, *15*(4), 457–476.

Jia, L., & Han, X. (2022). Tracing Weibo (2009–2019): The commercial dissolution of public communication and changing politics. *Internet Histories*, *4*(3), 304–332.

Khatsenkova, S. (2022, August 1). Racist videos of Africans fuel a million-dollar industry in China. *Euro News*. Retrieved August 10, 2022, from www.euronews.com/my-europe/2022/08/01/racist-videos-of-africans-fuel-a-million-dollar-industry-in-china

Kovács, J. (2002). Understanding the impact of TikTok: A study of TikTok's strategy and its impact on users' lives. In M. J. Sousa & C. G. Marques (Eds.), *Innovations and social media analytics in a digital society* (pp. 266–282). CRC Press.

Lash, S. (2002). *Critique of information.* Sage.

Lee, E. A. (2020). *The coevolution: The entwined futures of humans and machines.* MIT Press.

Li, Z. (2020, September 17). Ri huoyue yonghu po liuyi [Daily active users reach 600 million. *Jingji Ribao*, p. 9.

Li, Z. (2021, October 11). woguo jumin xiuxian shijian jiao yiqing qian yousuo zengjia [Chinese people enjoys more leisure time than that before COVID-19 pandemic]. *Zhongguo Lüyou Bao*, p. 1.

Litzinger, R., & Ni, Y. (2021). Inside the Wuhan cabin hospital: CONTENDING narratives during the COVID-19 pandemic. *China Information, 35*(3), 346–365.

Liu, M. (2018, April 19). Douyin zongcai cheng qianren shenhe tuandui meitian zengzhang [The censhorship team of TikTok is enlarging]. *Nanfang Dushi Bao.* www.sohu.com/a/228827322_161795

Liu, P., & Murphy, F. (2022, July 16). Kingsoft word processor scandal raises awkward questions for cloud firms. *Caixin Global.* Retrieved August 10, 2022, from www.caixinglobal.com/2022-07-16/kingsoft-word-processor-scandal-raises-awkward-questions-for-cloud-firms-101913847.html

Lu, X. (2020). Lessons from Weibo: Media convergence and contemporary Chinese politics. *Javnost-The Public, 27*(2), 126–139.

Ma, H., Meng, Z., Yan, D., & Wang, H. (2021). *The Chinese digital economy.* Palgrave Macmillan.

Mai, J. (2020, October 10). Wuhan communist chiefs praise city's "heroic" residents after plan to teach them to be grateful over coronavirus outbreak backfires. *South China Morning Post.* www.scmp.com/news/china/society/article/3074293/wuhan-communist-chiefs-praise-citys-heroic-residents-after-plan

Mathiesen, T. (2013). *Towards a surveillant society: The rise of surveillance systems in Europe.* Waterside Press.

Mcgregor, G. (2020, November 3). The world's largest surveillance system is growing. *Fortune.* Retrieved August 10, 2022, from https://fortune.com/2020/11/03/china-surveillance-system-backlash-worlds-largest/

Mosco, V. (2004). *The digital sublime: Myth, power, and cyberspace.* The MIT Press.

Negro, G. (2017). *The internet in China: From infrastructure to a nascent civil society.* Palgrave Macmillan.

Nichols, T. (2017). *The death of expertise: The campaign against established knowledge and why it matters.* Oxford University Press.

Rauch, J. (2018). *Slow media: Why "slow" is satisfying, sustainable, and smart.* Oxford University Press.

Repnikova, M. (2017). *Media politics in China: Improvising power under authoritarianism.* Cambridge University Press.

Schneider, F. (2018). *China's digital nationalism.* Oxford University Press.

Sun, L. (2022, May 5). Chinese splurge on Russian snacks. *South China Morning Post.* www.scmp.com/economy/china-economy/article/3169298/chinese-splurge-russian-snacks-ukrainian-food-show-solidarity

Svensson, M. (2017). The rise and fall of investigative journalism in China: Digital opportunities and political change. *Media, Culture and Society, 39*(2), 440–445.

38   *Yi Guo*

Tai, Z. (2006). *The internet in China: Cyberspace and civil society.* Routledge.
Tehranian, M. (2004). Civilization: A pathway or peace? *Globalisations, 1*(1), 82–101.
Tong, J. (2019). The taming of critical journalism in China: A combination of political, economic and technological forces. *Journalism Studies, 20*(1), 79–96.
Towey, H. (2022, July 11). Researchers in China claim they have developed 'mind reading' artificial intelligence that can measure loyalty. *Business Insider.* Retrieved August 10, 2022, from www.businessinsider.com/china-says-mind-reading-ai-can-gauge-politi cal-loyalty-reports-2022-7
Wang, F., & Lo, L. N. K. (2018). *Navigating educational change in China: Contemporary history and lived experiences.* Palgrave Macmillan.
Wang, H. (2016). *The transformation of investigative journalism in China.* Lexington.
Wang, H., Sparks, C., & Huang, Y. (2018). Popular journalism in China: A study of China youth daily. *Journalism, 19*(9–10), 1203–1219.
Wang, P., & Chen, X. (2019, September 26). 94.1% shoufangzhe dou youguo aiguoxin baopeng de chaoran shike [94.1% of the respondents had experienced moments in which their patriotic feelings overwhelmed]. *Zhongguo Qingnian Bao.*
Wang, R. (2015). Engaging government for environmental collective action: Political implications of ICTs in rural China. In W. Chen (Ed.), *Networked China: Global dynamics of digital media and civic engagement: New agendas in communication* (pp. 77–96). Routledge.
Weber, M., & Koehler, C. (2017). Illusions of knowledge: Media exposure and citizens' perceived political competence. *International Journal of Communication* (11), 2387–2410.
Wei, H. (2021, January 20). WeChat now an integral part of daily life in China, says survey. *China Daily.*
Wu, A. (2004). *Zhongguo dianzi zhengwu [Digital governance of China].* Renmin chubanshe.
Xi, J. (2022). Buduan Zuoqiang Zuoyou Zuoda Woguo Shuzi Jingji [Continue to Develop China's Digital Economy]. *Zhongguo Minzheng* (2), 4–5.
Xia, S. (2021). Amusing ourselves to loyalty? Entertainment, propaganda, and regime resilience in China. *Political Research Quarterly.* doi:10.1177/10659129211049389
Xie, E., Foxman, M., & Xu, S. (2021). From public sphere to magic circle: Playful publics on the Chinese internet. *Internet Histories, 5*(3–4), 359–375.
Xin, X. (2018). Popularizing party journalism in China in the age of social media: The case of Xinhua news agency. *Global Media and China, 3*(1), 3–17.
Xinhua News Agency. (2021, September 26). Xi sends congratulatory letter to 2021 world internet conference Wuzhen submit. *Xinhua Net.* Retrieved August 10, 2022, from www.xinhuanet.com/english/2021-09/26/c_1310210567.htm
Yan, A. (2018, September 3). See double? *South China Morning Post.* www.scmp.com/ news/china/society/article/2162540/chinas-newspapers-have-serious-case-deja-vu-over-african-summit
Yang, G. (2009). *The power of the internet in China: Citizen activism online.* Columbia University Press.
Yang, Q. (2022). Patriotic language and the popular use of history. In L. Jaivin, E. Sunkyung, & S. Strange (Eds.), *China story yearbook: Contradiction* (pp. 9–13). Australian National University Press.
Yang, T., & Fang, K. (2021). How dark corners collude: A study on an online Chinese alt-right community. *Information, Communication & Society.* doi:10.1080/13691 18X.2021.1954230

Yang, Y. (2022). TikTok/Douyin use and its influencer video use: A cross-cultural comparison between Chinese and US users. *Online Media and Global Communication, 1*(2), 339–368.

Yang, Y., & Ha, L. (2021). Why people use TikTok (Douyin) and how their purchase intentions are affected by social media influencers in China. *Journal of Interactive Advertising, 21*(3), 297–305.

Zeng, W., & Sparks, C. (2019). Popular nationalism: Global Times and the US-China trade war. *International Communication Gazette, 82*(1), 26–41.

Zhang, Y., Liu, J., & Wen, J. R. (2018). Nationalism on Weibo: Towards a multifaceted understanding of Chinese nationalism. *China Quarterly* (235), 758–783.

Zhang, Z. (2021, January 21). 'Malicious returnee'—mayor must carefully choose his words. *China Daily*. www.chinadaily.com.cn/a/202201/21/WS61ea6580a310cdd3 9bc8284b.html

Zhao, Y. (1998). *Media, market, and democracy in China: Between the party line and the bottom line*. University of Illinois Press.

Zheng, S. (2020, February 11). Wuhan's dancing coronavirus patients provide moment of light relief for Chinese looking to keep their spirits up. *South China Morning Post*. www.scmp.com/news/china/society/article/3050024/wuhans-dancing-coronavirus-patients-provide-moment-light-relief

Zhou, B. (2015). Internet use, socio-geographic context, and citizenship engagement: A multilevel model on the democratizing effects of the internet in China. In W. Chen & S. D. Reese (Eds.), *Networked China: Global dynamics of digital media and civic engagement: New agendas in communication* (pp. 19–36). Routledge.

Zhou, M. (2020, December 4). 'Innovation': The anxieties of our time summed up in one world. *CGTN*. https://news.cgtn.com/news/2020-12-04/-Involution-The-anxieties-of-our-time-summed-up-in-one-word-VWNIDOVdjW/index.html

Zuo, M. (2022, April 6). Coronavirus: Chinese people are dancing their thanks to pandemic workers. *South China Morning Post*. www.scmp.com/news/people-culture/social-welfare/article/3173232/coronavirus-chinese-people-are-dancing-their

3 Toward an Algorithmically Planned Economy

Data Policy and the Digital Restructuring of China

Brett Aho

After two decades following a laissez-faire approach to its tech industry, China has rapidly changed course and has entered into a new era of regulatory governance. Between 2019 and 2022, a series of new regulations and enforcement actions have marked a radical change in how the Chinese Communist Party (CCP) engages with its digital development. These actions include a volley of new laws, policies, legal actions, antitrust fines, product bans, guidelines and stakeholder workshops for actors in the platform economy and for the tech industry in general. Put together, they reflect a state that has begun to assert a high degree of authority over its digital development trajectory, effectively ushering in what appears to be a new era of government involvement in its digital civilization.

This chapter will describe the development of China's new digital development trajectory in four parts. The first section will begin by considering the official designation of data as a factor of production, examining what exactly that means in both theoretical and functional terms. Here we will examine how data is being gradually reconceptualized as a quasi-public good in order to increase data supply and circulation. In the second section, we will examine the architectures of China's new data ecosystem, which includes a series of new laws, policies and guidelines that together are reshaping digital development. Third, the chapter will turn toward China's SCS, a long-term project poised to shift China's regulatory state toward algorithmic governmentality. Finally, the chapter will close by considering how these policies together mark the beginning of a new era of algorithmic economics, with substantial implications for international political economy and beyond.

Data as a Factor of Production

In consecutive policy documents beginning in October 2019, the CCP has begun to identify and highlight data as a new factor of production (Central Committee, 2019; State Council, 2020; MIIT, 2021). In basic economic terms, factors of production can be regarded as the inputs to an economy

DOI: 10.4324/9781003299899-3

and are traditionally recognized as land (natural resources), labor and capital. In China, technology has also previously been recognized as a factor of production. These factors can be regarded as the building blocks of the economy—the resources that are used in order to produce goods and services, or outputs. Under communism, factors of production are said to belong to the people, rather than to a capitalist class, and are valued for their usefulness to the people rather than for the accumulation of profit. Since the establishment of China's Socialist Market Economy (SME) under Deng Xiaoping, factors of production have undergone substantial reform, and the state has demonstrated a dedication to market-based allocation. However, the CCP also continues to exercise a high degree of authority over factor markets.

Labor markets, for example, are controlled through the *hokou* system, which structures and limits labor mobility (Tombe & Zhu, 2019). Land markets are also controlled by the state, and revenues from sales of land use rights continue to be a primary source of infrastructure investment (Henderson et al., 2020). China's capital markets have undergone radical privatization and liberalization since the establishment of the SME, although regulation and state oversight remain present (Jiang et al., 2020). Technology markets operate with substantial state intervention, which include the implementation of technology transfer initiatives, technology parks, research and development initiatives, and the subsidization of various new technologies. Allegations of state-sponsored industrial espionage may also be worth mentioning (Hvistendahl, 2021).

The type of authority that the state exerts over factor markets is perhaps best exemplified by an April 2020 opinion adopted by the State Council, practically titled "On Building a More Complete System and Mechanism for Market-based Allocation of Factors." The document prescribes a cautious relaxation of factor markets, while at the same time increasing state supervision. Reforms include more flexible land use management, a relaxation of certain *hokou* restrictions and an "orderly expansion of the financial industry to the outside world" (State Council, 2020). These gradual, supervised prescriptions reflect a measured approach to economic policy reforms, characteristic of Deng Xiaoping's philosophy of "crossing the river by touching the stones."

When it comes to data however, state intervention in factor markets appears a bit more bold. Under the heading "Accelerating the cultivation of the data element market," the State Council first calls for open sharing of government data resources for public use and the promotion of data sharing and exchange between regions and departments. Here, the state leads by example, announcing the opening up of its own data resources. The document also decrees an expansion of data collection, as well as the standardization of data use in a wide range of industries. This explicitly includes data use in agriculture, industry, transportation, education, security, urban management and public resource trading. Finally, the document calls for the accelerated development of standardized data management and classification systems, as well as privacy protection and security. Together, these first steps of China's intervention in data factor markets seek to promote the orderly establishment of a formalized data economy while also increasing data supply and circulation.

The recognition of data as a factor of production lays the groundwork for the CCP to make decisions about how data is allocated and gives the state the authority to manage how data circulates through its economy. In theory at least, it also implies that data should be treated as a resource that belongs to the people and that it should be used first and foremost to advance the interests of the collective, rather than the interests of a capitalist class. To this end, the state has gradually introduced a series of policies that incrementally shift how data is conceptualized by policy makers. Around the world data is typically conceptualized as either a resource or a form of capital to be collected, owned and controlled by private actors (Sadowski, 2019). However, it appears as though China seeks to challenge these entrenched notions by gradually gaining access to the immense data stores currently managed by China's tech giants. The actions taken by the CCP suggest a shift in how data is conceptualized—from a private good toward a quasi-public good.

Going back to basic economics, a public good by definition is both non-excludable and non-rivalrous. Excludability is a characteristic of private ownership, referring to the ability to restrict access to a good, so a non-excludable good is something that users cannot be blocked from using. Rivalry refers to the exclusive use of a good, such that a non-rivalrous good is something that can be used by multiple different actors without impacting the ability for other actors to use it. Data is fundamentally non-rivalrous, as it can be copied and used by multiple different parties without impacting supply. However, at the moment, most data is currently treated as excludable. Organizations maintain their own data silos and are rarely driven to make data available to the public.

Take, for example, a hypothetical dataset that contains the location of all individuals who purchased a new bassinet in the last year. This dataset, which would roughly correlate to the locations of newborn infants, might provide valuable insights to a wide range of organizations. Advertisers could use the data to market ad-space for other infant products. Companies that produce children's products or toys might use the data to re-think their brick and mortar strategy. Urban planners might use the data to plan where to place future playgrounds or schools. Environmental health policy makers might consider how to steer pollution away from areas with high densities of fragile newborn lungs. Childcare providers might use the data to plan for the opening of new daycares. In all cases, the use of this dataset by one actor does not diminish its ability to be used by another. It is therefore fundamentally non-rivalrous. However, should this hypothetical dataset be controlled exclusively by a private company like Taobao, then it remains excludable. Under these circumstances, Taobao alone would be able to benefit from the operationalization of the data. Even though making this data public might provide social and economic stimulus to society as a whole, there is little incentive for the data owner to do so.

This excludability is precisely what the CCP seeks to challenge. As described by Chen (2022), "Underlying these sweeping top-down efforts to put data to work is the idea that economic efficiency would be enhanced at a societal level if data can flow to economic agents who make productive use of it." By rendering more data public and by increasing data flows, the state seeks to maximize the social and economic benefits that data can provide. Broadly speaking, it seeks to gradually challenge the dimensions of exclusivity by default which act as a barrier to economic development. By developing policies designed to encourage the circulation and flow of data, the CCP aims to maximize data network effects, which can stimulate high-quality economic growth (Prüfer & Schottmüller, 2021).

The conceptual transformation of data is perhaps most clearly reflected in the Central Cyberspace Affairs Commission's (CCAC) 14th Five-Year Plan for National Informatization. This high-level planning document lays out the CCP's priorities for digital development for the period from 2021 to 2025, which are primarily centered around the development and mobilization of data resources. The guiding ideology of the CCAC (2021) plan notes: "with deepening supply-side structural reform as the main line, we will further liberate and develop digital productive forces, accelerate the construction of a new economic structure with the great domestic circulation as the principal aspect" (p. 10). Again, by conceptually labeling data as a factor of production, the state asserts its authority to reshape how data is allocated. When it comes to the cultivation of data factor markets, the plan lays out three main projects:

1. *Strengthen data factor theory research: Research the perfection of the nature of property rights based on the nature of data, and build data property rights frameworks oriented toward stimulating industry development. Explore data value assessment systems, and research the perfection of data value assessment frameworks.*
2. *Establish and complete effective data circulation structures and systems: Accelerate the establishment of basic structures, standards, and norms for data resource property rights, trading and circulation, cross-border transmission, security protection, etc. Explore the establishment of uniform and standardized data management structures, and formulate mechanisms for data registration, assessment, pricing, transaction tracing, and security inspection.*
3. *Cultivate standardized data trading platforms and market subjects: Establish and complete data property rights trading and sectoral self-discipline mechanisms. Develop systems for data asset assessment, registration and settlement, transaction matching, dispute mediation, and other such market operations.*

(CCAC, 2021, p. 22)

The plan also includes substantial investments toward the construction of data infrastructures, all with the broad goal of increasing data flows. This includes the digitization of a wide range of public services, including power grids, railways, highways, water, aviation, logistics and so on. Leading by example, the plan includes a range of open government data sharing initiatives, including the construction of a nationwide public data platform. This includes the sharing of data held at all levels of government (CCAC, 2021, p. 50). As for privately held data, the plan is a bit more cautious, noting that the state will "encourage enterprises to open up data on search, e-commerce, social interactions, etc." (CCAC, 2021, p. 22).

This encouragement has already begun. One of the first companies targeted for data sharing has been Ant Financial—China's largest collector of consumer financial data. Initially, the company resisted pressure from the People's Bank of China (PBoC), which sought access to the company's data stores in 2020. However, after a series of escalating sanctions, including the mysterious disappearance of company founder Jack Ma and a $2.8 billion antitrust fine for parent company Alibaba, the company bowed to pressure and agreed to open up its data stores to state authorities (Yu & Mitchell, 2021). Today, Ant's consumer financial data has been integrated with a centralized government credit reporting system. The PBoC itself has called data collected by platforms a "public good," which should be more strictly regulated (Yu, 2021). A similar fate befell ridesharing app Didi Chuxing, the largest such service provider in China. After resisting demands to share trip data with state authorities, the company also faced a series of harsh crackdowns, culminating in the issuance of a $1.2 billion fine by the CAC for violation of data laws (Zhong & Yuan, 2021). As noted in an editorial published in the state-operated Global Times: "The state will never allow tech giants to collect more detailed personal information in their mega-databases than the state has of the Chinese people" (Global Times, 2021).

All of this is not to say that all of China's data will be made freely available to any and all actors but rather that the state will gradually seek to increase the circulation of data through the development of new data sharing platforms, markets and protocols. In the cases of Ant and Didi, the companies' data silos have been pried open in order to provide access to state actors—however mandated data sharing with private actors is not yet part of the picture. The aforementioned national informatization plan, however, will encourage private actors to circulate their data by developing new data exchange infrastructures intended to lower transaction costs for organizations that might be convinced to engage in data sharing programs. To support more effective data exchange, authorities have also begun to develop data classification systems and protocols intended to standardize security and privacy (SAMR, 2021; DSL, 2021, Article 19). However the state still faces many challenges. Fair pricing mechanisms will need to be developed in order to ensure that companies remain invested in the development of new data collection capacities.

A New Digital Ecosystem

In his 2018 characterization of China's tech sector, Kai-Fu Lee employs the term "gladiatorial arena," describing a cutthroat business atmosphere where firms used whatever means necessary to provide themselves with an edge over their competition (Lee, 2018). This resulted in a tech culture where intellectual property rights were rarely enforced and where innovations were often quickly copied and modified. In part because of this hyper-competitive atmosphere, China's tech sector flourished, sparking rapid sectoral growth. This hands-off approach is perhaps best exemplified by the 2016 Supreme People's Court case *Qihoo 360 v. Tencent*. The case involved an escalating tit-for-tat between two tech companies seeking to achieve market dominance in anti-virus software. This included behavior such as blocking user access to competitor content and services, fabricating news stories about competitors, publicly accusing competitor's software of spying on users, ad hominem attacks on firm leadership and the rollout of updates that blocked competitors' products from functioning. The case concluded with a ruling that stated that no company had market dominance and therefore they could not have abused their market position. Eventually, the two companies were ordered by the Ministry of Industry and Information Technology (MIIT) to stop fighting; however, the ruling did nothing to curb cutthroat behavior within tech competition, essentially affirming the law of the jungle within tech competition.

Since 2020, all of this has begun to change. Under the banner of "common prosperity," China has shifted its economic development priorities from high-speed growth to high-quality growth. Changing tack, China has begun to take a proactive role in its digital development and is now taking efforts to shape the trajectory of its digital civilization. As stated by Xi Jinping in an October 2021 speech to the Politburo: "All countries are competing to formulate digital economy development strategies and roll out encouraging policies; the development of the digital economy is rapid, it radiates broadly and the depth of its influence is unprecedented." In the speech, Xi explicitly acknowledges that the laissez-faire approach has led to problems. He elaborates:

> [O]ur country's digital economy has displayed several unhealthy and unregulated symptoms and trends in its rapid development; these problems not only influence the healthy development of the digital economy, but also violate laws and regulations; they constitute threats against the country's economic and financial security, and must be firmly corrected and dealt with.
>
> (Jinping, 2021)

In a subsequent speech published in Qiushi, the official CCP theory journal, Xi also makes it clear that global competition is a major motivating factor behind new policy developments:

> All countries are competing to formulate digital economy development strategies and roll out encouraging policies; the development of the digital economy is rapid, it radiates broadly, and the depth of its influence is unprecedented. It is becoming a critical force in reorganizing global factor resources, reshaping global economic structures, and changing global competition structures.
>
> (Jinping, 2022)

After two decades exerting only a light touch over its tech development, China has definitively begun to play regulatory catch-up. The flurry of new policies includes the Anti-Monopoly Guidelines for the Platform Economy (Feb 2021), the Data Security Law (Sep 2021), Critical Information Infrastructure Security Protection Regulations (Sep 2021), Guiding Opinions on Strengthening Overall Governance of Internet Information Service Algorithms (Oct 2021), Personal Information Protection Law (Nov 2021), Internet Information Service Algorithm Recommendation Management Regulations (Dec 2021), the 14th Five-Year Plan for National Informatization (Dec 2021), updates to the Anti-Monopoly Law (Jun 2022) and the Outbound Data Transfer Security Assessment Measures (Sep 2022). In addition, the state has begun to ramp up enforcement of existing regulations; this includes the enforcement of labor laws, as well as a crackdown on deceptive business practices such as fake reviews or product misrepresentation.

Another tool increasingly used to exert control over tech development is the expansion of so-called golden shares in tech companies. In brief, a golden share provides a state actor with a minority stake in a company along with a board seat and a controlling vote in shareholder meetings. Golden shares effectively provide the state with veto power over company actions, as well as the ability to direct and steer business decisions and corporate planning. Feng Chucheng, a partner at the Beijing-based consultancy Plenum, describes these shares as "A Sword of Damocles hanging over the heads of firms that have them" (Yang et al., 2021). The precise extent to which the government owns and exploits golden shares in Chinese tech companies is unknown, although it is estimated to be fairly extensive. University of Hong Kong Law Professor Angela Huyue Zhang estimates that the China Internet Investment Fund (CIIF), which is effectively owned and operated by the Cyberspace Administration of China (CAC), invested in over 40 Chinese tech firms between April 2020 and May 2022 (Zhang, 2022). The CIIF's portfolio of controlling shares now includes Weibo (Chinese Twitter), ByteDance (parent company of TikTok), SenseTime (advanced AI), Kuaishou (short video streaming), Full Truck Alliance (logistics) and Ximalaya (podcasts). Many online news aggregators have also sold stakes to government-related entities, including Yidian Zixun, Qutoutiao and Sina News.

In many recent policy documents, the term "ecology" or "ecosystem" (生态) has become increasingly prominent, reflecting the holistic approach that the nation is taking toward its digital development (Creemers & Triolo, 2022). This concept is emblematic of how the state seeks to create a digital ecosystem that encompasses all aspects of society. High-level digital policy planning documents not only focus on the tech industry but also include digital development planning for universities, trade associations, research institutes, local governments, public health institutions, public utilities, rural areas and beyond. Part of this holistic approach to digital development also includes various forms of digital social governance. For example, citing growing video game addiction among children, in 2019 the National Press and Publication Administration (NPPA) limited video game use for children to 90 minutes on weekdays and three hours on weekends. These limits were subsequently tightened in July 2021, allowing children only one hour of gameplay per day on weekends, with gaming companies subject to inspections to ensure compliance. In addition, the NPPA also initiated a nine-month freeze on the granting of licenses for the publication of new video games, resulting in an estimated 14,000 game developers going out of business, as reported by the state-run periodical *Securities Daily* (Ye, 2021). State media has consistently referred to video games as "poison" or as "spiritual pollution," terms which have previously been employed within the national bans on pornography (Mei, 2018, pp. 28–31)

When viewed together, these policies reflect a state that has begun to assert a commanding role in the development of its digital ecosystem. Xi Jinping (2022) describes the broader aims of China's flurry of new tech policies as an effort to prevent the expansion of platform monopolies and the "disorderly expansion of capital"; he calls for the development of market access structures, fair competition inspection and "comprehensive, multilevel, three-dimensional" oversight structures, including complete oversight of "entire chains and entire areas before, during and after events." This expansion of state oversight aligns with the designation of data as a factor of production and the reconceptualization of data as a quasi-public good. Comprehensive oversight structures imply data surveillance and provide the state with the ability to better understand and conduct social and economic governance. This oversight is also integral to the ongoing development of the SCS.

The Social Credit System

The development of China's data ecosystem is happening in tandem with the development of the SCS, which is currently positioned to be one of the chief instruments of China's digital regulatory state—a centralized authority which oversees compliance with established laws, rules and behavioral norms. In brief, the SCS is a massive information processing platform, collecting and compiling data streams from a wide range of sources, which together reflect the behavior of a particular actor. By algorithmically processing data streams, the system outputs a series of scores which reflect how well or how poorly that actor has behaved. A good credit score means that the actor has behaved in accordance with a set of rules and norms prescribed by the state for that particular actor. On the other hand, a bad credit score means that an actor has failed to behave in accordance with the parameters set for them. The scores are applied to all economic actors and include both individuals and firms. Individuals may see their credit scores lowered if they are caught engaging in behavior deemed "antisocial," such as jaywalking, littering, fighting or buying too many video games. Firms may see their credit scores lowered if they are late on tax payments, engage in unethical business practices, cause environmental damages or fail to comply with regulations. On the other hand, actors may see their scores raised if they participate in voluntary programs, state-sponsored initiatives or engage in other prosocial behavior as determined by the state.

Many of the new tech policies mentioned in the previous section have been formulated to support the continued development of the SCS. The classification of data as a factor of production essentially provides the state with the authority to oversee and manage the nation's data flow, and the reconceptualization of data as a quasi-public good helps to expand data circulation and supply, accelerating the quantity and quality of data streams available for the operation of SCS. The flurry of new tech policies (including informatization, data security and golden shares) all support the development of the SCS, which is premised on the system having access to as much of the nation's data as possible. The more data the system can access, the more effectively it can operate. The aforementioned integration of Ant's consumer financial data with the PBoC's centralized credit reporting system in 2021 is a logical first step. The company is China's largest financial services corporation and the second largest in the world after Visa. Financial transaction data has been proven to be an incredibly rich source of information, and can be processed to create a fairly comprehensive image of how both individuals and firms operate and behave (Zuboff, 2019).

The scores provided by the system carry with them certain rewards or punishments, specifically tailored to incentivize compliance. These carrots and sticks might include the adjustment of tax rates, the increase or reduction of bureaucratic red tape, acceleration or denial in permitting processes, access to foreign travel visas, public procurement processes, fines, blacklisting and so on (Aho & Duffield, 2020). Further, these rewards and punishments can be algorithmically tweaked and modified in order to adjust for maximum effect. In addition, the system can apply a different set of rules for a different set of actors. For example, if pollution is causing environmental issues in a particular region, the SCS parameters might be shifted to incentivize local industries to invest in pollution reduction measures. If the state wants to discourage tobacco or video game consumption, it can ding individual credit scores for such purchases. If a particular industry or subset of the economy is struggling, the SCS can prescribe virtual deregulation or can artificially inflate credit scores to provide targeted economic support. With every action taken by the system, data is collected to observe the effect of the intervention, allowing the system to algorithmically learn and adjust future interventions to maximize desired effects. The longer the system is in operation, the more effective it becomes.

SCS should thus not be simply regarded as an instrument for individual social governance but should be understood as a flexible and dynamic instrument that allows the CCP to better manage and regulate the Chinese economy. As a result of explosive growth over the past decades, China has struggled to rein in a substantial range of unethical business practices (Ang, 2020). Part of this can be tied to the fact that law is conceptualized very differently in China than in the United States or Europe. In Confucian thought, a society governed by laws is evidence of a breakdown of social harmony; as Confucius himself is quoted, "a plethora of new laws, a proliferation of minute regulations, amendments and amendments of amendments . . . for a society, compulsive lawmaking and constant judicial interventions are a symptom of moral illness" (Leys, 1997, p. 176). Rather, modern China is a society in which many essential functions are not fundamentally premised on laws and a strong judiciary. Rather than "rule of law," Chinese society follows a "rule of man" approach, in which governance functions through effective public administration and moral bureaucracy (Frederickson, 2002). Again, this can be seen in the aforementioned dispute between Qihoo 360 and Tencent, which resulted in the Ministry of Industry and Information Technology simply telling the two firms to stop misbehaving. Jiao (2004) describes this difference in terms of formal and informal social control systems, noting that as a result of the deeply embedded influence of Confucianism and Taoism, law is regarded as "secondary to collectively held moral principles" (p. 126).

Again, the development of the SCS is perhaps best understood as a uniquely Confucian means to help solve many of the social and economic woes that plague China. The system does not function on the basis of law but instead encourages good behavior through a process of "self-regulation" (State Council, 2014). Oftentimes, this is interpreted in the Anglophone world negatively as a form of coercion, which reflects an ontological divide between US/European and Chinese conceptualizations of governance; Americans and Europeans are accustomed to a strong legal system with concrete parameters for lawful behavior and specific punishments for unlawful behavior. In a society where "rule of law" dominates and concepts of governance are couched in legal terms, novel quasi-legal methods of governance are difficult to grasp. With the SCS, the boundaries of acceptable and unacceptable are less concrete, and punishments for bad behavior are tied to a score rather than to the behavioral act itself.

The SCS is fundamentally based on the expansion of a surveillance state, which is another aspect of the digital development trajectory this chapter seeks to outline. Data surveillance is part and parcel of China's official recognition of data as a factor of production, as well as the gradual reconceptualization of data as a quasi-public good. These policies allow the state to develop a bird's eye view over the nation's data circulation, which also provides it with a bird's eye view over the nation's economy, and perhaps to a slightly lesser extent, a bird's eye view over the nation's social and political dynamics. While the expansion of the surveillance state may raise alarm in the West, state surveillance has a long history in China. As David Lyon (2003) observes, "Since at least the fourth century BC, China has kept accurate population records and limited the movement of her citizens from home. It is hardly surprising that new technological means are sought to update old practices" (p. 74). With the founding of the PRC, the *Danwei* system operated as the state's primary surveillance and social governance infrastructure (Bray, 2005). Although the *Danwei* gradually declined in relevance since the market reforms of Deng Xiaopig, in many ways the SCS is now taking its place, re-empowering the state with an updated tool to mobilize society in the advancement of national political projects. Kostka (2019) finds that many citizens are unconcerned about the surveillance and control aspects of SCS because they already assume that state security apparatus have access to any and all information already (p. 22).

Toward an Algorithmically Planned Economy

With a bird's eye view over the economy, along with an advanced AI system that can flexibly tailor interventions designed to modify firm and individual economic behaviors, China is on its way to becoming the world's first algorithmically planned economy. As noted by Jack Ma, founder of the Alibaba Group and the wealthiest man in China:

> Over the past 100 years, we have come to believe that the market economy is the best system, but in my opinion, there will be a significant change in the next three decades, and the planned economy will become increasingly big. Why? Because with access to all kinds of data, we may be able to find the invisible hand of the market.
>
> (Global Times, 2017)

Today, the ongoing development of the SCS can be seen as a harbinger of this significant change.

Part of the failure of economic planning during the 20th century was that the state lacked effective and accurate data collection and processing capacities. These barriers have since been eliminated. Chinese citizens now produce more data than any other country, thanks to a high level of smartphone adoption, rapid adoption of mobile payments and the widespread use of superapps (Lee, 2018). With steady increases in data processing capacities, alongside the continued development of artificial intelligence/machine learning (AI/ML), the potential for effective economic planning has expanded. As this chapter has demonstrated, data policies and frameworks are being developed which provide the CCP with a high level of oversight over the immense quantity of data streams that flow through China's increasingly digital society. Together, these data streams reflect the social and economic behaviors of all actors, both firms and individuals. The SCS is being designed with the capacity to observe these data streams and process them into outputs (credit scores), which should then result in a change in future data streams. It operates as a governance system that can coordinate dynamic interventions in the economy with real-time feedback. An algorithmically planned national economic system is not only technologically feasible but is arguably already under construction.

Interestingly, the concept of an AI-planned economy is something that has also been explored in Chinese science fiction. Han Song's *2066: Red Star over America*, published in the year 2000, portrays a future where China is governed by a powerful AI system named "Amanduo" that manages society in a manner that maximizes personal happiness. The story tells of how "the Americans refuse to submit to its control and soon witness their country's downfall, but the Chinese people indulge themselves in joyful dreams when Amanduo creates a new 'harmonious society' in the land of the old middle kingdom" (Song, 2013, pp. 87–88). Interestingly, by coincidence, the same term, "harmonious society," is also frequently and prominently employed in State Council planning documents for the SCS. As the introduction to the 2014 Planning Outline states: "accelerating the construction of a social credit system is an important basis for comprehensively implementing the scientific development view and building a harmonious Socialist society" (State Council, 2014, p. 1).

The origins of the SCS can be found in the CCP's adherence to systems engineering, an interdisciplinary academic field that focuses on the design, management and integration of complex systems (Hoffman, 2018). After its emergence in the 1950s and 1960s, the discipline faded in popularity in the United States and Europe but continued to expand in China, such that it is now a mandatory subject for party cadres in Beijing at the CCP's Central Party School (Hvistendahl, 2018). Systems engineering methodologies are at the core of the SCS, which itself can be regarded as a system of systems. With over 47 institutions involved in its development and construction, the system brings together a wide range of pre-existing legal and regulatory infrastructures, and has been steadily expanding since the publication of the 2014 State Council Plan (Drinhausen & Brussee, 2021). Eventually, the system aims for comprehensive oversight, allowing the CCP to overcome challenges to centralization posed by a massive population distributed over a large country. Standardized data protocols, expanded data sharing infrastructure and the construction of national data platforms all contribute to the coming-together of the county's many systems. Indeed, one of the basic principles of the national informatization plan is to "uphold the entire country as one chessboard" (CCAC, 2021, p. 11).

The ability of China to consolidate its digital development onto a single chessboard is likely to provide the CCP with substantial competitive advantages when steering the country's economic development in the globalized economy. While most democratic nations appear likely to continue coordinating industrial policy through complex and often-opaque processes involving power dynamics between rent-seeking corporations, civil society and state actors, China instead is positioned to adopt a more data-driven process. This does not however necessarily predict future Chinese economic dominance. The effectiveness of a centralized algorithmically coordinated economy remains untested, and the system still faces countless implementation challenges. In many ways, the United States is also slowly moving toward an increasingly algorithmically mediated economic system, albeit with powerful corporations in the driver's seat (Phillips & Rozworski, 2019). Irregulation coupled with an expansion of business models premised on the commodification of behavioral data and algorithmic governmentality has proven to be effective drivers of innovation and economic growth (Zuboff, 2019). Elsewhere, economic development is not treated as the most important factor informing the construction of a digital civilization. The EU's General Data Protection Regulation (2016), Digital Markets Act (2022) and Digital Services Act (2022) together prioritize the ethical dimensions of digital development and seek a healthy balance between diverse economic, socioeconomic and moral interests. As societies around the world continue to follow diverse and divergent approaches to digital development, certain social and economic trade-offs will become increasingly clear.

This chapter has sought to provide a rough outline of China's current digital development trajectory. As it has demonstrated, China has begun to take bold steps to control how new technologies are being woven into the fabric of society. While datafication is poised to have profound effects on human societies around the world, the nondemocratic, authoritarian power structures of China have allowed it to take a uniquely proactive approach in shaping how its data revolution unfolds. This is aided by a flexible Marxist socialist ideology, which has allowed the CCP to assert its authority over the nation's data flows by identifying data as a new factor of production. As China moves forward with its development of its new digital ecosystem as well as the consolidation of data streams through the SCS, the country is increasingly poised to begin experimenting with new algorithmic economic systems. AI is poised to be one of the great transformational technologies of all time, with societal implications on par with the agricultural or industrial revolutions. At this critical moment in technological development, it is important to consider how these revolutionary forces are being channeled and woven into the fabrics of society.

Works Cited

Aho, B., & Duffield, R. (2020). Beyond surveillance capitalism: Privacy, regulation and big data in Europe and China. *Economy and Society, 49*(2), 187–212.

Ang, Y. Y. (2020). *China's gilded age: The paradox of economic boom and vast corruption.* Cambridge University Press.

Bray, D. (2005). *Social space and governance in urban China: The Danwei system from origins to reform.* Stanford University Press.

Central Committee. (2019). Decision of the central committee of the communist party of China on several major issues concerning adhering to and improving the socialist system with Chinese characteristics and promoting the modernization of the national governance system and governance capability. *Fourth Plenary Session of the 19th Central Committee of the Communist Party of China.* www.12371.cn/2019/11/05/ARTI1572948516253457.shtml

Central Cyberspace Affairs Commission (CCAC). (2021). *The 14th five-year plan for national informatization* (R. Creemers, H. Dorwart, K. Neville, & K. Schaefer, Trans. It was J. Costigan & G. Webster, Eds.). https://digichina.stanford.edu/work/translation-14th-five-year-plan-for-national-informatization-dec-2021/

Chen, Q. (2022). China wants to put data to work as an economic resource—but how? *Digichina.* Stanford Cyber Policy Center. https://digichina.stanford.edu/work/china-wants-to-put-data-to-work-as-an-economic-resource-but-how/

Creemers, R., & Triolo, P. (2022). *Analyzing China's 2021–2025 informatization plan: A DigiChina forum.* https://digichina.stanford.edu/work/analyzing-chinas-2021-2025-informatization-plan-a-digichina-forum/

Data Security Law (DSL). (2021). *Data security law of the people's republic of China.* www.npc.gov.cn/englishnpc/c23934/202112/1abd8829788946ecab270e469b13c39c.shtml

Drinhausen, K., & Brussee, V. (2021). China's social credit system in 2021. *MERICS China Monitor.* https://merics.org/en/report/chinas-social-credit-system-2021-fragmentation-towards-integration

Frederickson, H. G. (2002). Confucius and the moral basis of bureaucracy. *Administration & Society, 33*(6), 610–628.

Global Times. (2017, June 14). Can big data help to resurrect the planned economy? *Global Times.* www.globaltimes.cn/content/1051715.shtml

Global Times. (2021). Huanshi Rui Commentary: Why is the state's request for Didi Chuxing to be removed from the shelves for rectification? Retrieved from https://opinion.huanqiu.com/article/43o4K21Rxr5

Henderson, J. V., Su, D., Zhang, Q., & Zheng, S. (2020). *The costs of political manipulation of factor markets in China.* CEPR Discussion Paper No. DP15247, Available at SSRN: https://ssrn.com/abstract=3688201.

Hoffman, S. (2018). Managing the state: Social credit, surveillance and the CCP's plan for China. *AI, China, Russia, and the Global Order: Technological, Political, Global, and Creative, 42.*

Hvistendahl, M. (2018, March 14). A revered rocket scientist set in motion China's mass surveillance of its citizens. *Science.*

Hvistendahl, M. (2021). *The scientist and the spy: A true story of China, the FBI, and industrial espionage.* Penguin.

Jiang, F., Jiang, Z., & Kim, K. A. (2020). Capital markets, financial institutions, and corporate finance in China. *Journal of Corporate Finance, 63,* 101309.

Jiao, A. (2004). The integration of formal and informal social control in China. In *Broadhurst, Roderic G (2004) crime and its control in the people's republic of China.* Proceedings of the University of Hong Kong Annual Symposia 2000–2002.

Jinping, X. (2021). Making solid progress toward common prosperity. *Qiushi Journal.* http://en.qstheory.cn/2022-01/18/c_699346.htm

Jinping, X. (2022). Unceasingly make our country's digital economy stronger, better, and bigger. *Qiushui Journal* (R. Creemers, J. Costigan, & G. Webster, Trans.). https://digichina.stanford.edu/work/translation-xi-jinpings-speech-to-the-politburo-study-session-on-the-digital-economy-oct-2021/

Kostka, G. (2019). China's social credit systems and public opinion: Explaining high levels of approval. *New Media & Society.* https://doi.org/10.1177/1461444819826402

Lee, K. F. (2018). *AI superpowers: China, Silicon Valley, and the new world order.* Houghton Mifflin.

Leys, S. (Ed.). (1997). *The analects of Confucius.* W.W. Norton & Company.

Lyon, D. (2003). 4 Cyberspace, surveillance, and social control. *Asia. com: Asia encounters the Internet, 67.*

Mei, Z. (2018). *Pornography, ideology, and the internet: A Japanese adult video actress in Mainland China.* Rowman & Littlefield.

Ministry of Industry and Information Technology (MIIT). (2021). *"14th Five-year" plan for the development of the big data industry.* Etcetera Language Group trans. Center for Security and Emerging Technology. https://cset.georgetown.edu/wp-content/uploads/t0426_big_data_plan_EN.pdf

Phillips, L., & Rozworski, M. (2019). *The people's republic of Walmart: How the world's biggest corporations are laying the foundation for socialism.* Verso Books.

Prüfer, J., & Schottmüller, C. (2021). Competing with big data. *The Journal of Industrial Economics, 69*(4), 967–1008.

Sadowski, J. (2019). When data is capital: Datafication, accumulation, and extraction. *Big Data & Society, 6*(1), 2053951718820549.

Song, M. (2013). Variations on utopia in contemporary Chinese science fiction. *Science Fiction Studies, 40*(1), 86–102.

State Administration for Market Regulation (SAMR). (2021). *Guidelines for internet platform categorization and grading—draft for comment* (Stanford Cyber Policy Center, Trans.). https://digichina.stanford.edu/work/translation-guidelines-for-internet-platform-categorization-and-grading-draft-for-comment-oct-2021/

State Council. (2014). *State council notice concerning issuance of the planning outline for the construction of a social credit system (2014–2020)* (R. Creemers, Trans.). https://chinacopyrightandmedia.wordpress.com/2014/06/14/planning-outline-for-the-construction-of-a-social-credit-system-2014-2020/

State Council. (2020). *Opinions of the central committee of the communist party of China and the state council on building a more complete system and mechanism for market-based allocation of factors.* www.gov.cn/zhengce/2020-04/09/content_5500622.htm

Tombe, T., & Zhu, X. (2019). Trade, migration, and productivity: A quantitative analysis of China. *American Economic Review, 109*(5), 1843–1872.

Yang, Y., Leng, C., & Zhu, J. (2021, Dec 15). Fretting about data security, China's government expands its use of 'golden shares.' *Reuters.* www.reuters.com/article/china-regulation-data-idCAKBN2IU2B7

Ye, J. (2021, December 31). China gaming crackdown: Freeze on new video game licences extends into 2022 as 14,000 gaming-related firms shut down. *South China Morning Post.* www.scmp.com/tech/policy/article/3161717/china-gaming-crackdown-freeze-new-video-game-licences-extends-2022

Yu, S. (2021, March 2). Jack Ma's Ant defies pressure from Beijing to share more customer data. *Financial Times.* www.ft.com/content/1651bc67-4112-4ce5-bf7a-d4ad7039e7c7

Yu, S., & Mitchell, T. (2021, April 23). China's central bank fights Jack Ma's Ant Group over control of data. *Financial Times.* www.ft.com/content/1dbc6256-c8cd-48c1-9a0f-bb83a578a42e

Zhang, A. (2022). China's golden tech grab. *Project Syndicate.* www.project-syndicate.org/commentary/china-regulatory-crackdown-tech-firms-golden-share-ownership-stake-by-angela-huyue-zhang-2022-05

Zhong, R., & Yuan, L. (2021, August 27). The rise and fall of the world's ride-hailing giant. *New York Times.* www.nytimes.com/2021/08/27/technology/china-didi-crackdown.html

Zuboff, S. (2019). *The age of surveillance capitalism: The fight for a human future at the new frontier of power.* Profile Books.

Index

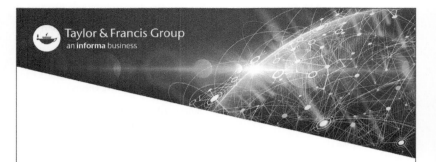